Dear anyone who has low self-esteem,

You're absolutely beautiful. Your smile is amazing. Wear it more often.

I love you.

—Keishorne Scott

LIFE

Keishorne Scott

Foreword by Chris Broussard of ESPN

I dedicate this book, *LIFE*, to the millions of you who are at a crossroads in your LIFE. For those of you who ever lack confidence, self-esteem, and motivation. To everyone out there with poor self image and poor quality friends who aren't there to see you through hardship and adversity, to the millions of people with insecurities who believe they're not good enough to be successful, happy, or loved. I want you to know that things aren't always as bad as they seem, and that you can overcome anything. *You're absolutely amazing!*

LOVE. INSECURITIES. FRIENDS. ENVY

LIFE

ACKNOWLEDGMENTS

First, I would like to thank God, because without Him, this book would never have been created. I trust Him in everything I do. A relationship with God is the most important relationship you can have. Trust Him and everything will always turn out fine. Always remember, God doesn't send you problems you can't handle, or people you can't face.

Second, I would like to thank Cheryl Meredith; without her constant love, support, and encouragement, none of this would have been possible. I'll always love you, Buddafly.

I would also like to thank my mother and father, who have always believed in me, and Frantz Debrosse Jr., my good friend for LIFE, who has always stood by me. Thank you.

Thanks to Christian "Chrissy" Bryant, my editor, who brought her craft, passion, literary magic, and good character to this book and made it shine.

Last, I would like to thank Cheryl Wills, Chris Broussard, Tony Gaskins Jr., Kimberly Hudson, Harold Reed Jr., Shaniquewa Lino, Rossmery Gomez, Adonica Edwards, Miss Rain King, Jalishana Olivierre, Raquel Williams, Deborah M. Yearwood, Sasha Singh, Godwin Reid, Wendy Henri, Angel Allen, Al Rodriguez, Dania Rodriguez, Tony Rodriguez, Nigel Contaste, Hans Monfiston, Jamaal DeVore, Sean L. Brereton and everyone else who helped me on this awe-inspiring journey. Thank you for your continuous love and support. I love you all.

CONTENTS

Foreword

For all those who worry about the younger generation, who complain about our "directionless youth," who fear that we have no responsible young men to lead us in the future, I present to you Keishorne Scott.

Keishorne Scott is driven. He's responsible, he's committed, and he's focused on what's right. But perhaps most impressively, Keishorne Scott is transparent. That is what makes *LIFE* such a tremendous book—its transparency. In it, Keishorne pours out his soul. With refreshing honesty and uncommon candor, he tells it like it is, like it should be, and like it can be.

LIFE has lessons for all of us, but especially for teenagers and twentysomethings. Scott speaks with the wisdom of an elder but in the language of a young man. It's a rare and captivating combination, one that enables him to reach a generation that many others with his understanding cannot motivate. Scott sympathizes with their challenges, fears, and obstacles, but encourages them to overcome. In fact, he presents himself as an example—as proof that they can overcome, that they must overcome, that they will overcome.

Chris Broussard
ESPN

1

LOVE

I have found the paradox, that if you love until it hurts, there can be no more hurt, only more love.

—Mother Teresa

"Love" is a problematic term on its own. We use it to indicate everything from preferences (*I love hot dogs*) to appreciation (*I love the way you arranged those flowers*) to emotion (*I love my dog*) to commitment (*I will always love you*). We use "I love you" to apologize (*I know I upset you, but I didn't mean to—please forgive me*), to make demands (*do this because you love me*), to make promises (*I will take care of you for the rest of your LIFE*), or to avoid a promise (*I love you, isn't that enough?*). Love is expressed in many ways and comes in many forms. It is as varied and unique as the individuals who give and receive it.

Unconditional Love

Unconditional love is the sincere love, the love that lasts forever. This kind of love comes when you have found the person you are destined to be with. Nothing can destroy unconditional love. Arguments or disagreements don't bother you because your love overcomes everything. When we add "unconditional" to qualify love, we narrow the possible range of meanings considerably. If you really comprehend what forms a "condition," you will find that the type of love that is truly unconditional is one with which we are not terribly familiar in our culture.

What does "conditional" mean? *Conditional*—relating to conditions. *Conditions*—circumstances or requirements. So, if the presence of love relates to any particular condition (circumstance or requirement), it is not, by definition, unconditional. Unconditional love is not based on personal attributes. If you love someone for his or her personality or sense of humor, the way the person makes you feel, or any other characteristic, your love is conditional. It depends on the presence of that characteristic. If the person ceased to be or have all the things that you enjoy, would the love remain?

Love based on sex is not unconditional. It depends on sexual attraction between the participants. It is possible that two people who have a sexual relationship may also love one another; the test of this is whether the love would be present if the sexual relationship ended and both parties moved on. If this circumstance would interrupt the love, then the love is not unconditional. The love of friends is not unconditional. It depends on shared interests, mutual support, communication, and all the other things that make our friends our friends. People who share friendly love may also love one another unconditionally. If the love is unconditional, it remains present even through betrayal, lies, long periods of no communication, and severe divergence of lifestyles and interests. If any of these circumstances threaten the love, then it is conditional.

The major thread among all of these is that love must *grow* to become unconditional. It is impossible to love someone unconditionally unless you have first learned to love that person with conditions. The conditions are what produce the love, but as the conditions change or fade, they are also what prove the love.

We all talk about how in love we are with our partners. After analyzing and brainstorming what exactly love is. I decided to use questions to help. If they lost their sight would you still be there? If they lost their hearing would you still be there? If they needed a kidney and you were the only match would you give it? How about if they were paralyzed tomorrow? What if they couldn't have children? What if they lost a limb? Etc. The next time you tell your partner you "love them," remember this.

—Deborah M Yearwood

MY SHORT LOVE STORY

I was in love before, and yes it felt amazing, so I didn't regret it. It felt like the world was chanting, "Keishorne...Keishorne...Keishorne..." and I was waving my hands as though I were on a float at the Macy's day parade. Being in love is a tremendously great feeling; it really was, especially when I was getting Love in return. I can't remember exactly when I fell in love; it was like remembering the first thing I saw when I was born. But I definitely remember those feelings—those looks that made me feel like I was at the top of the world!

I am not in that relationship anymore, but I remember the first time I introduced myself to Cheryl. She was in a hurry and running fast to catch the Kingsborough Community College *cheese* bus to head home. I had been observing her from a distance and, for a while now, I had been bowled over completely with her beauty. But today, somehow I couldn't control my emotions. My body was not in control of my mind; my heart had all the power. I ran up to her and said, "Hi, my name is Keishorne, and you are?" She smiled. "I'm Cheryl," she said, sounding like an angel. I said, "Nice to meet you, Cheryl."

We smiled, spoke briefly, and then went our separate ways. I wanted to see her all the time, wanted to be with her, but how? I didn't know who she was and what she did? Lost in my thoughts about her, I got the shock of my life when I saw her in school the following day and got her AIM screen name before class in the Clusters of Kingsborough. It was the happiest moment of my life. We said hello to each other and spoke for a couple of minutes. But this time, when we said bye to each other, I wasn't sad. Now I knew where to find her, so I was only looking forward to the next day when we would meet again.

Our friendship slowly started gaining momentum. She had also taken an interest in me, which made my heart rate elevate. We wrote poems back and forth, decorating them with a smiley face here and a "lol" there—you know, the gushy stuff. Things got better as time passed. November 11, 2007, was the day we made it official to call ourselves a couple, and it was a great feeling; she was my queen. Yes, our love was very positive, with nothing but smiles and laughter as we enjoyed life and every minute together. To make a long story short, I asked her to marry me on February 14, 2010 at Mr. Chows Restaurant in Manhattan, New York. That night was spectacular! I went home late that night and went straight to meet my mom. I sat down on her bed and told her, "I'm in love, and it feels like the world just stopped to acknowledge it." She cried with me and said, "That's what love does."

A few months passed and things started degrading. My negative attitude kicked in and it started ruining our relationship. For the first time, I wasn't giving her the love and attention she had been accustomed to all this time, and I stopped appreciating her, as well, which I had been doing since we met. I started changing. And I wasn't only hurting her, but my family and friends as well. I was turning into a very stupid boy. I guess I got what I deserved; she left me during the first quarter of 2011, and when I tell you I broke down, I mean I couldn't eat, sleep, breathe, smile, love, or laugh anymore. I was hurt and devastated. My heart was shattered into many little pieces.

I desperately needed help. I needed spiritual help. That's when God stepped in and whispered in my ears that he had better plans for me. A year ago, I wasn't the way I am now. God has changed me. I was once the most hardheaded hypocrite individual in the world, but God has transformed me into a completely different human being. He had seen my relationship with my loved ones become estranged, so he took the fool out of me and broke me down completely only to get the *King* out of me. This was how he planned to see me. If my friends knew me back then they knew who I was, and I apologize for being like that. Now, I am a new creature, a completely different Keishorne Scott. I have buried my past. Looking back at it now only highlights my success and my relation with the almighty! And one reason why God created time was to ensure that there would be a place to bury the failures of the past. We cannot get stuck in our past. We have to refuse to go back. I love the man I'm becoming now. I really do. As I tell everyone, don't judge me by my past. I don't live there anymore.

Love is the most common emotional feeling. It drives a person to continue living. It is the foundation of life to become emotionally mature and to achieve belongingness.

FOR THOSE WITH A BROKEN HEART

Stop being angry about what you've lost or who left you or who isn't there anymore. Stop being upset and sad because you feel like you wasted your time with someone who broke your heart. This only makes you weak! It happened! So, no, it's not a dream; it's real. He/she is gone! Heartbreak's a teacher. It's ok to cry, it's ok to be angry, and it's ok to grieve and be upset. It's ok. But just don't stay there! Never allow one person to paralyze you! I know it's hard; trust me I do. I'm going through it right now. But we have to keep moving forward. We have to keep hope alive in ourselves. *Stop being upset at what you've lost and start getting excited about what you got coming*! It's time to let go and move on! We cannot have hope for the past! We can only have hope for the future.

LOVING YOURSELF

One of the most important things I've learned throughout my years is that in order to love others, I must first love myself. This self-love is the foundation of self-respect and allows me to love others. Loving yourself means having a relationship with yourself and knowing that you are important. I am not speaking about loving your physical body, although that is important too. I am referring to a deeper connection beyond the physical body you now reside in. It implies that you understand that you are one with God and not separate from Him. It also means that you are one with love and not separate from this positive emotion. This truth has also led me to the conclusion that LIFE is too short for anger, worry, or anything other than love. It only takes one instance of losing someone you love for you to truly understand this. Few things survive the storms and trials of LIFE, except love.

When you first meet people, you want to know all about them and get to know them. You want to know their likes, dislikes, and values. You recognize when they are feeling good or when they are hurt or unhappy. You come to respect, admire, and appreciate them. You support and encourage them. You go out of your way to accommodate them. How awesome would it be if you could do this for yourself? You are just as important and valuable as other people are. Invest in yourself even more than you invest in others.

> *You can't do better than you're doing now*
> *if you don't do better than you're doing now.*
>
> **—Hans Monfiston**

I always say, we have to respect those who respect themselves. We *must* have self-love in order to get love in return. I love myself, with all my flaws and imperfections. I have learned to feed love and starve hate. Remember, if someone doesn't love you, that's perfectly fine. Nobody in this world can love you better than you love yourself, so don't let anyone treat you any worse than you treat yourself, and don't expect everyone to know how to treat you, either. Show them by the way you treat yourself. But you should never give in to superficial things that eventually cause you to lose your self-love—superficial things such as lust. We need to understand that lust is shallow, but love is deep; the best time to love is now, because love is timeless. I will discuss this later on in the chapter. For now, tell yourself, "I am me, I love myself, I accept myself, and those who judge my exterior will find it harder to know my interior."

Stop looking for other people to complete you.
Find yourself & you will see that you are whole.

—♥ Kimberly Hudson

"What is love?" is one of the most frequently asked questions, but the possibilities are infinite. Many people do not know the value or meaning of love. *Love is patient, and love is kind. It does not envy; it does not boast; it is not proud. It does not dishonor others, is not self-seeking, is not easily angered; and it keeps no record of wrongs. Love does not engage in evil, but rejoices with the truth. It always protects, always trusts, always hopes, and always perseveres,* explains 1 Corinthians 13 4:7 in the New International Version Bible. Whether it's love for a relative, a friend, or a lover, or just the love of living, it's really what you intend it to be deep within yourself. Whomever you choose to love, the how and why, are what matter most. You'll know you love someone when you care about the person's well-being. You'll know you love someone when you question your own obsessive actions. You'll know when you feel it deep inside your heart, body, and soul that it's certainly not infatuation, but pure, genuine, natural love. You'll feel more alive than ever before. There is no such thing as a perfect love, but when you love someone, everything will seem perfect.

"Love" has become more a word void of emotion than an action from the heart. While hate comes easily, love takes courage and develops over time, becoming stronger. *I love you* is the most overused, misunderstood, and abused phrase in the English language, in my opinion. This is why most don't really understand what it is or what its capabilities are. Love is tangible, very powerful, but it can also be weak, very similar to our hearts. Few experiences hurt more than a broken heart, when you love someone and that person doesn't love you in return. Because of how strong it is and how vulnerable it can make us, our love must be guarded and not carelessly handed out.

We need to come together and love each other, care for each other, and protect each other. To get love, we have to give love, right? Love knows no reasons. Love knows no lies. Love defies all reasons. Love has no eyes. Love is not blind; it sees, but it doesn't mind. Love is so easy to feel, but so hard to explain; easy to get, but so hard to let go; easy to spell, but difficult to define. Love is not created by words, but by feelings; not by humans, but by hearts. Love is better expressed in deeds than in words, because actions do speak louder than words.

I believe that when you cry for the person you love, the real tears aren't the ones that fall from your eyes and cover your face, but those that fall from the heart and cover the soul. I don't consider myself an expert or someone who knows where to find love, but here's what I know: if we are willing to open up to a higher presence, we will realize that we don't really know it all, especially when it comes to love. And that is okay, because love doesn't care if you know it. It will always find a way to make you realize that you had it all along. It will always find you, especially when you least expect it.

Love can also be a contradiction. It's hard to find but easy to lose; makes you feel good, but hurts you so bad; opens your eyes, but makes you blind; fills up your heart, but rips it apart. It is like air: you can't see it, but you can feel it. You have got to be open to experience everything it has to offer if you want to get its full benefit. If you've never had a broken heart, it will be difficult to appreciate a healed heart full of love. This is why some take love for granted. If you've never been blinded by it, how can you be grateful when you see the small things that make love so worthwhile? Open up to love and it can teach you many things in many ways. Never regret the bad, only look forward to the good, knowing it will surely come.

At the touch of love everyone becomes a poet.

—Plato

Love is a crazy thing, because it has no limits. There is no telling how far or wide love can go; love makes you do the craziest things. Love can be twisted and molded into various forms. It can be your guiding motivation or your ultimate end. It can be your reason for living or your reason for dying.

I thought I was in love many times, but I have come to understand that it wasn't love at all. I felt love for that person, but I wasn't *in* love. Growing up, I was very confused about the definition of love. I thought love was one thing and one thing only, that one thing everyone was searching for, but then I came to understand that love has no limits and can be many things. As I said before, the possibilities are infinite. I came up with my own definition of love a while back, which is pretty funny, but it works. I believe that love is when you no longer question your emotions. Love is real, so when you don't consistently ask questions like, "Is this the right person for me?" or "Can I spend my whole LIFE with this person?" that is when you can probably say that you are in love. Love is when you know everything is just right and you know in your heart that the person you have chosen feels that same exact way as well.

Love is when three years go by and you look back and say, "Wow, it's been that long already?" Love is when you just can't get that person out of your mind. Love is when you are willing to change your ways just to make that person happy. When you go to sleep, your loved one is always in your dreams. He or she is the first thing on your mind when your day starts and the last thing when it ends. You find yourself thinking or talking about your loved one to random people for no reason at all, and the only explanation for that is love—but before we can love anyone, we must first love ourselves.

LOVING OTHERS

We've all heard that it is difficult, if not impossible, to love others if we don't first love ourselves. But do you know that your ability to love others will strengthen the love you have for yourself? It will also teach you LIFE lessons that can make you a better person, if you allow it. Your love for others will show you things about yourself that are hidden and would not otherwise surface. It will stretch you, empower you, anger you, humble you, and strengthen you.

Loving people requires giving them the freedom to be whomever they choose to be, in whatever way they choose. It doesn't mean you want them to do what you want. Love isn't molding people but accepting them. Love is allowing people in your LIFE to make their own choices. It is a noble act that requires you to give of yourself, offering your faith, trust, and loyalty. The more you love, the more you give a part of yourself and accept more of others. You don't become less of who you are, but you understand that love requires sacrifice. Love doesn't need to stand in front of us to be recognized. If it's too far for the eyes to see, it has power strong enough for the heart to feel.

We have to learn to make the most of what LIFE offers us each day, because we never know what tomorrow may bring. Make the most of today, it's your gift to use. Don't live in the past or long for the future; instead, live for making the now even greater. Love everyone, and learn to forgive and forget. We don't forgive people out of weakness; we forgive to display our strength. Forgiveness means that we understand that people make mistakes, including ourselves. If we can plant forgiveness into people's lives, regardless of whether they "deserve it" or not, we will reap that same forgiveness when we make mistakes. We need to love each other, learn to forgive, and choose to forget. Yes, we all make mistakes and need forgiveness at one point or another. Remember this when you are tempted to hold on to bad feelings. We often blame our mistakes on others when in fact we have the power to control our own actions. The way we do things and react to them is our responsibility and no one else's.

Forgiveness is not foolishness. If people don't treat you with love and respect, then they don't deserve you. They don't deserve your time and they definitely don't deserve the energy required to hate. Don't hate others; let them bury themselves in their own insecurities and hatred. In general, people tend to hate too often and too easily. If you want to love, then love hard. Fall in love with yourself. Eliminate any destructive self-criticism, be kind and positive, forgive yourself, and learn to appreciate yourself more than ever. If you love someone else, tell that person; don't wait until it's too late to do so, because tomorrow is never promised. Refusing to forgive can cause you to stray away from love and fall into the crowd of confused people who look for love in the wrong places and for all the wrong reasons. Both those who hate you and those who love you should motivate you. Those who love you will motivate you through their support and their expectation to see you succeed. Those who hate you should motivate you to prove their assessment of you wrong. You can use love as a catalyst and hatred as fuel. Both love and hate can positively impact you if you allow them to.

Don't spend time with anyone who doesn't cherish you or understand your self-worth. Love yourself enough to protect your heart. Be wise who you lend it to, and don't cry it out for someone who doesn't respect you. I truly believe that wisdom is what helps you decide what you want and what you need. Sometimes those things we desperately want is not what we need and wisdom will guide us into making good decisions, if we allow it. This applies to relationships especially, because love is at its strongest and weakest when it comes to those we love. Guarding your heart means being able to see traits in people that complement you, help you be the best you can be, and uplift you, instead of just pleasing your eyes. It is not wise to totally ignore what you like either, but be aware that your heart is at stake and that love is not like a switch you can turn off and on.

Love should definitely direct you toward happiness. The happiest people don't necessarily have everything; they just make the best of everything that comes their way. They handle circumstances knowing they cannot control everything but willing to do all they can to make them better. Perspective is very important. How you view yourself, those around you, and the special one you love will either help you attain happiness or make it seem far off. If all you can see is negativity and sadness in your LIFE and in those you love, your relationships cannot be happy. They will never be happy if you have that type of attitude. You will have to work on changing your perspective before happiness can come freely. Happiness will come when you decide what to keep and what to let go. Use your wisdom to guide your love, and your love to lead you to happiness, in every area of your LIFE.

Thanksgiving is essential to happiness and to love as well. Happiness comes to those who cry, those who hurt, those who have searched, and those who have tried and failed but still continue to try, for only then can they appreciate the importance of people who have touched their lives. We should count the things we have instead of the things we don't. Take time to count your blessings rather than making complaints. Enjoy every day as if it's your last, and stop revisiting the past. If the past calls, push the ignore button because it has nothing new to say. Do you ever notice this cycle in your relationships? When you are thankful for what your mom, sister, brother, and lover do, it encourages them to do more and shows them you appreciate them. However, complaining about their shortcomings or areas in which they need improvement does nothing but add to the problem. Thanksgiving is the antidote to pain and is required for happiness, including thanksgiving for yourself. Be thankful for your talents, gifts, and ability to help others. Be thankful that you love yourself and can love others. Be thankful and watch how your perspective changes.

LOVE OR LUST

Some think I'm "soft" because I respect women. What they fail to realize is that I'm stronger! Truth is, you cannot destroy me! I'm stronger because of the smile I put on my face. I'm stronger because I actually use my brain. And I'm stronger because I'm blessed. And the only thing that's weak is the energy you give towards their hate!

—Frantz Debrosse Jr.

Lust is the desire of the flesh, and love is a necessity for the heart. Lust is that feeling that you get when you first see someone you are attracted to. Some people think that they have experienced love at first sight, when really all it can be is lust. You want that person's body. You are attracted to their flesh. You think that person is attractive, which can lead you to believe that you love him or her. This can be confusing. Desire can truly convince a person that they are in love. Attraction can take place on many levels: physical, intellectual, circumstantial, and others. The point is that lust is a feeling that is easily confused with love because we tend to express these feelings in almost identical ways. Both genders can pursue someone for either lust or love by spending time, sending gifts, or other acts of kindness. Love is when you truly know someone inside and out and can love that person despite his or her flaws. The person is important to you, and you know that you would do anything for him or her. You want to make that person happy, no matter the sacrifice required on your part.

People also mistake lust for true love because they have a conception of what they want, or because they don't know what they want. Then they try to mold the other person into that conception, and they disregard certain things that don't fit in. They may see red flags as they date or spend more time with a person, but because of their desire for that person's body and their misunderstanding of what love is, they ignore these things to continue on in a relationship. Something inside is trying to tell them that they are latching on to the wrong person and that perhaps a great friendship could develop, but a loving relationship just isn't going to happen.

Another scenario that often happens when lust is mistaken for love is that the people actually begin to change themselves. Instead of trying to mold the object of their affection, they begin to mold themselves. It is important to compromise in any relationship, and we cannot be resistant to change if we want the best in LIFE. But when you have to change someone or yourself in order for a relationship to work, that is not love. If that is happening, you should ask yourself what the motivation is behind your actions. Are you trying to help someone overcome a drug or alcohol addiction? This would fall into the category of *Love is patient, love is kind, love endures all…* Or are you trying to make someone lose fifteen more pounds because you think that person is unattractive, while he or she feels fine? This motivation is selfish and is therefore not love. Lust can motivate people to do destructive and demeaning things to other people. Always make sure you check your motives in addition to your feelings. Feelings can be deceptive while motives will really tell us what is in our hearts. This is the major difference between love and lust. You should not expect anything from people that you are unwilling to give yourself. And if you cannot love them for whom they are, what they look like, the extra weight they may carry, or the pimples on their face, you don't love them. When you are willing to walk away from a person or a relationship for any reason other than that the person hurt you, question if you love that person. Love endures and lust walks away. Attempting to shape someone into what you want him or her to be is selfish and indicates that you only love yourself.

Love is LIFE and LIFE is to love. I love LIFE and I adore living in it.
—Keishorne Scott

In my first year of college, I met a girl and she was the definition of fine. I mean her body was beautiful. I thought it was love at first sight but later realized it wasn't love at all. After talking with the girl for a few months, I came to the conclusion that it was lust and that all I really wanted was her body, not her mind. This experience taught me something: that the sexiest thing about a woman isn't always her body but her mind and intellect. It's about the way she talks, the way she walks, the way she carries herself, and the confidence she displays. It is more than her face; it's what's inside her head. Beauty is always refreshing, but I am sure we can all agree that it will not weather the ups and downs of relationships. Neither is it a solid foundation upon which a relationship can stand.

We need to focus on what is real and what is essential in LIFE, as well as what we can learn from it. Love is real and essential. Love gives and lust takes away. Love is selfless and lust is selfish. Fall in love when you are ready and not when you are lonely, because someday someone will walk into your LIFE and make you realize why it never worked out with anyone else. Love is worth the wait and definitely should not be shortchanged for lust. Love yourself enough not to rush into relationships based on lust. They will often turn out hurtful and cause pain. Love is worth any pain it comes with; lust causes pain without any benefit except a lesson learned.

In my experience, when someone loves you, the way that person says your name is different. You just know that your name is safe in that person's mouth. She or he will speak LIFE and positive things to and about you. She or he will not defame or belittle you in public or private. She or he will become your greatest cheerleader and will push you even when you want to give up. Lust has never produced these types of results, and we should all be wise about distinguishing between love and lust, for our heart's sake. I have learned that love only talked about can be easily turned upside down, but love demonstrated is irresistible.

True love never dies for it is lust that fades away.
Love bonds for a lifetime but lust just pushes away.

—*Alicia Barnhart*

PRIDE

Too much pride will destroy you

—Proverbs 16:18

Pride is the enemy of any relationship. Stubbornness, controlling behavior, and refusal to forgive are all just pride in disguise. Allowing these and other pride-filled reactions into your relationship can undermine the foundation of your relationship and quickly sabotage any efforts you make toward building a solid future together. Recognize pride immediately, and refuse to allow it any place.

I realize that no relationship is unbreakable. But if you are in love and things start falling apart, step up to the challenge and put your pride aside to make things work. Adversity brings out the true love in a relationship or exposes vulnerability. Fight for what is yours even if it hurts. Put your pride aside to make your love grow. Remember that pride is the most precious thing owned by the loneliest people. Loving relationships are not about how much love you have in the beginning but about how much love remains until the end. Love never walks away! People do. Choose who is worth chasing after and who is worth letting go, but don't allow pride to blur your decision. God will always give you the people you need: to help, build up, love, and allow you to become the person you were meant to be. Sometimes just being a friend is the only way to stay close to someone you love, and it may be the best role you can play in their lives.

It is always good to have pride, I will never dispute that, but there is such a thing as having too much pride. This we can call "pridefulness." It's great to "protect" yourself from others; however, when you find someone who truly loves you, it's okay to let your guard down. It is okay to look within yourself and realize you don't need to control every situation. You should always say sorry when you know you have hurt or mistreated another person.

Pridefulness should not be confused with the healthy traits of self-confidence, dignity, and honor. Those are very different types of pride and are not related to what we are discussing here. You can have pride in your country, the accomplishments of loved ones, and a job well done, for example. But that doesn't make you a prideful person. And remember that you can be confident and secure without being controlling, stubborn, and unforgiving. These manifestations of pride hurt those around you—and ultimately you as well—as they ravage your relationships. If you are guilty of needing to have the last word and be the final authority on issues relating to family, home, finances, the children, or other issues that come with any relationship, then you are exhibiting controlling behaviors. Such behaviors will quickly sabotage any chance of happiness you might have had in your relationships. While you may have the best intentions and really want to help, that is not how behavior is received. It communicates that you think you are smarter, more astute, more capable, or more talented than your partner. It can demean their contribution to the relationship and signify that you don't see him or her as your equal. It is degrading, often humiliating, and your partner will ultimately withdraw because his or her needs are not being met and the relationship is offering fewer and fewer benefits. Not many people want to stay where they feel unappreciated, insignificant, and worthless. On the other hand, if you are the one who feels these things, take time to talk with your partner. Don't allow your pride to prevent a frank discussion about how you feel. It is highly probable that the other person does not even realize how his or her behavior makes you feel. It is also likely the other person was brought up in an environment that taught these behaviors or has seen them in play somewhere else. Let's face it, we all make mistakes.

Proud people often commit relationship suicide by holding things back or hiding feelings that they are too proud to reveal to anyone, including their partners. Appearing to be strong, with great self-esteem, they are actually weak. Instead of dealing with pain they build walls to shield themselves from it. They are dishonest not only with their partners but with themselves. We are all human. We all need help from time to time, and no one is all-powerful. Anyone who believes otherwise is probably proud. Proud people should question why they are even in a relationship. Relationships of all types require compromise and honesty. The proud person is both dishonest and unwilling to compromise. You can see now that this type of behavior is very counterproductive to a healthy relationship.

When it comes to relationships, people should relate to and respect one another as equal partners. It is also good practice to put yourself in the other's shoes from time to time. A partnership only works when both partners feel loved, appreciated, respected, and valued. Each individual must feel free to have input, to offer opinions and suggestions, and is entitled to have them taken into account in the decision-making process. Each person should be recognized as an asset to the relationship. For example, if you are the primary wage earner in the family, be very careful that you do not assume more power than or exercise dominion over your spouse. A healthy marriage, friendship, or any other relationship is a careful balancing act in which both people contribute to the future direction of the partnership and both are highly regarded for the unique and necessary gifts they provide. Don't assume that the partner whose "gift" is to earn the family's income is somehow entitled to a greater share of power in decision-making. It is also poor judgment to assume that this person's contribution, though tangible, is what keeps the relationship together. That is as silly as saying that money is what makes relationships work. The stay-at-home mom who keeps the clothes clean and morale high is also very valuable; she is making a huge contribution. In your relationships, remember that you are partners and each of you is affected by the decisions of the other. Be respectful, encourage discussions, value one another's opinions, and be careful to make more joint decisions than unilateral ones.

Wake up, be real, and take advantage of the love you have in LIFE! Regardless of the roles you play, being prideful can cheat you out of many great things in LIFE. Remember that pride is hard and love is soft; you will need to assess whether or not you are allowing your own past experiences to blur or distort how you receive things from your friend, lover, or coworker. To love and be loved is a gift; not everyone receives that gift in LIFE. Stop being cocky and accept other people's feelings as real and justified. Recognize and come to terms with your weaknesses. You cannot always be right, nor is your way always the right way. Your beliefs are your opinions, but be open to others' opinions and learn sometimes. Put off any proud ways you have before you lose what could be the best thing that will ever happen to you. Pride is very subtle yet very costly.

Pride, often disguised as stubbornness, indicates that you care more about yourself than you do about the other person and denotes a lack of maturity. It can lead to controlling behaviors. This characteristic can potentially destroy a relationship.

Farah Averill, "Top 7: Ways to Improve Your Relationship,"

#7 SHOW APPRECIATION

Remember when you first started dating, how you used to go that extra mile to impress your partner? One of the essentials to a lasting and fulfilling relationship is to continue to *actively show* appreciation for your partner. They cannot read your thoughts. While you don't have to necessarily "pull out all the stops" the way you did when you first met, regular efforts to show your appreciation will do wonders for improving your relationship.

If you're not sure where to start, begin by giving them daily **compliments**. Tell her she looks amazing, or thank him for their attention-to-details when he reminds you to call your mother. The only rule is to make sure that you genuinely mean what you say. Make a habit of this and it will become a part of who you are and your relationship. Every plant needs water. Water your relationship with compliments that come from your heart and express genuine appreciation.

#6 CONCENTRATE ON THE PRESENT TO ENSURE YOUR FUTURE

Interestingly enough, the ability of your relationship to weather tough times has a lot to do with the amount of time you invest in it now. Unfortunately, over time and for a variety of reasons, many couples drift apart. When the storms come, as they will, their relationship is not strong enough to survive. To build a rock-solid relationship, start by acknowledging rather than ignoring the ordinary moments in your relationship. If your partner wants to share something she's reading on the Internet, for example, take a minute to **listen**, even if you simply grunt or gesture in response. It may sound strange, but if you accumulate enough of the little things, when you really need your partner, you'll find they are there for you. Don't take the present for granted, and you can prepare for a good future.

#5 SHARE POWER

When a man is not willing to share power with his relationship partner, John Gottman's research indicates there is an 81% chance that his relationship will self-destruct. While hoarding power may have gotten you ahead in your **career**, this strategy will backfire in your relationship. The ignored partner will feel like their opinions aren't valuable and how they feel doesn't matter to you. Stop this behavior immediately. People will only stay where they are undervalued for so long before they find someone else who will value them. To help save your relationship, develop a more compromising attitude. Practice by giving in on issues you don't feel extremely invested in. This is a good place to start, but you will have to deal with yourself and undo the thinking that makes you feel always in the right, always in control. Could this be insecurity, or even pride?

#4 FIND COMMON GOALS

A study conducted in collaboration with a dating site in the UK found that 13% of couples reported no longer having the same goals. This situation represents a ticking time bomb, as research has shown that couples with common dreams and goals have longer-lasting, more **satisfying relationships**. If you feel like you've been out of sync lately with your partner on this front, discuss your philosophy of LIFE together. The aim is for both of you to share what you want your LIFE to be about, where you want to end up, and what these things mean to you. Look for anything that's common between the two of you and talk about ways to work toward that aspiration together. This will also help you spend time together pursuing these goals and leave less room for distractions or for distance to get between you.

#3 UNDERSTAND ANGER

While outbursts of anger are common even in healthy relationships, when **anger** becomes an entrenched part of your relationship, you should be concerned. Sue Johnson, master therapist and pioneer of emotion-focused therapy, an empirically validated treatment for distressed relationships, refers to anger as a secondary emotion. Her theory holds that other (primary) emotions, such as sadness or a fear of being abandoned, can be found behind an angry front.

Think back to the last argument you had with your partner and use this new knowledge to look for hidden messages in what you and your partner were trying to communicate. Attempting to disregard the angry tone you both used, and try to tune in to what you were each saying. This can expose the true culprit and you can begin to work on the issue together. For instance, "You're a workaholic!" might really mean "I miss you and want to spend more time with you." Think about it.

#2 FOCUS ON WHAT'S FIXABLE

As long as an argument doesn't leave you feeling like you've been through an emotional roller coaster, consider it fixable. A study by economist Jay Zagorsky finds that 33% of couples have seriously divergent views on income, wealth, debts, and that **finances** is a major area that causes tension in relationships. In particular, the initial stages of living together can be especially vulnerable to monetary issues and expose concerns. So that this problem doesn't spiral out of control, everyone should sit down with their loved one and craft a detailed action plan before moving in together, making a commitment to share your finances. Know who will pay what, and what type of plan you have in case one of you is unemployed unexpectedly. This is a major issue in relationships but can be handled with care with proper planning. If you notice something wrong with your spending habits or how your partner handles the finances for the household, you should immediately consult with one another to see what you can do help get your finances on track. Go back to the agreement you made before you moved to solve any conflicts. Make sure this is a mutual decision and each person has an opportunity to voice concerns. Compromise. If changes have to be made, so be it. LIFE is ever changing. But remember that you should both be able to live with the new arrangement or it won't work. Use this method to address any other problems in your LIFE that you deem fixable. From communication to sex, parental responsibilities to the annual vacation, talk to one another.

#1 ACCEPT THE UNSOLVABLE

According to relationship scientist John Gottman, 69% of relationship conflicts are persistent problems. Unfortunately, they are usually the same issues that resurface no matter how long you've been together. If you find a problem seems to bring out painful **emotions**, you're dealing with a persistent issue. To stop this from ruining your relationship, you'll need to address the bigger issues underlying them. Take turns discussing with your partner what this loaded issue really means to you. Be willing to pull back the layers to get to the real problem. When your partner is talking, your job is to listen, be nonjudgmental, and find something from their perspective that makes sense to you. When it's your turn to talk, they should be doing the same thing. By treading more gently into touchy areas, you should at least be able to agree to disagree or make some small concessions for one another. But there will always be things in relationships that remain unsolvable. We all have different personalities. What do you do with these unsolvable issues? Ask yourself if they are too large for you to overcome. Some things are deal breakers, and no matter how many times you discuss them, they will always cause pain and bad feelings; these are things that you have to walk away from.

LIFE is simple; it's just not easy.

LIFE

LIFE may not always be as good as it should be, but it's never as bad as it could be. At the end of the day, you either focus on what's tearing you apart or on what's holding you together, and to tell you the truth: everyone has problem. If you don't have problems, you don't exist. Just listen to me: LIFE isn't always easy, but when you have God, everything is okay.

—Keishorne Scott

I remember back in 2006 when I was down and sad for a few weeks because I couldn't find a job. It seemed like the hardest thing for me to do. Either they said no or they said, "Thank you, I'll review your application and give you a call to let you know," which is the long way of saying no. I cried day and night until my body hurt and I couldn't move, until one day I got down on my knees and prayed. I prayed for hours and cried until I had no more tears to shed. I woke up the next morning energized, blessed, and ready to overcome whatever obstacle came my way. I dressed well, went to the city, and got me a job in the first retail store I went into. I was not lucky, I was *blessed*. We have to believe in ourselves and go after what we really want out of LIFE. We must have faith, hope, and belief in ourselves; to survive in this lifetime, we need all three. We need to worry less and pray more and forgive people and forgive ourselves, not because it's the right thing to do but because it makes us a better person. It makes our Lives even brighter. LIFE is much better when we are happy. I love better when my LIFE is better, my smiles are bigger when my LIFE shines brighter, and my mind is clearer when my heart loves longer. You see, a lot of us make choices for all the wrong reasons; we think that having a nice car, having money, sex, and popularity are the standards of living the good LIFE. We forget to see the real beauty in LIFE: the smiles, the happiness, the joy, the love, the people, the rights, and the wrongs. That's LIFE and that's living. Enjoy what you can today, because tomorrow we may not be here.

When life gives you a hundred reasons to cry, show life that you have a thousand reasons to smile.

LIFE can be tough at times, but we have to keep our head up and keep on pushing. The more we let little things bother us, the less we enjoy LIFE. Let your negative emotion be temporary; you're not obligated to be mad all the time for things that don't even make sense. Don't allow minor things to get in your way and make you feel less than yourself. Brush them off and live. Every day is your day. Leave all the drama, the pain, the negativity, and the self-doubt behind. Every day is a new day with new air, new seconds, new minutes, and new hours. You've become a new you since yesterday. Remember, what you need to know about the past is that no matter what has happened, it has all worked out to bring you to this very moment. And this is the moment you can choose to make everything new. Right now! LIFE is too short to deal with selfish, unworthy people. We should live LIFE to the fullest and be happy always, because you never know what can happen unexpectedly. Who wants to live a LIFE full of drama or unhappiness? Some friends and lovers may come and go, just to teach us when and how to let go. If they couldn't hold up in your past, they sure don't deserve your future. Never second guess yourself; if people are bringing you down with their negativity, remove yourself from the negativity and surround yourself with positive people who bring you support and love.

Stop letting others bring you down to their level. Refuse to lower your standards to accommodate those who refuse to raise theirs.

BE INDEPENDENT

I honestly believe that what holds most people back is always depending on other people. Most of us are lazy: we lack ambition, we lack drive, and most of all we lack character and self-esteem. We are so afraid of failure that we won't even take the risk to follow our dreams. That's why we settle, and then we complain about our standards in LIFE. We are comfortable being uncomfortable, and just being average.

When I stand before God at the end of my life, I would hope that I would not have a single bit of talent left, and could say, "I used everything you gave me."

—Erma Bombeck

Sometimes the closest people to you are the ones you're best without. I learned that the hard way. You have to distance yourself from certain people, not because you don't love them but because you have to move forward with your LIFE. You can't always rely on other people to do things for you or help you advance every single minute, because one of LIFE's greatest pains is disappointment. You need to learn to stand on your own two feet. If you are hungry, get your own plate; if you are thirsty, fill your own glass; quit always depending on people to do things for you. Nothing will be given to us easily.

In LIFE you need to look around you and see if the people at your side really deserve to be there. Do they motivate you? Uplift you? Inspire you? Love you or be real with you? Choose your entourage wisely, and only hang around the type of people and participate in the activities that you are comfortable with. Remember, everybody doesn't deserve a seat at your table. As I always say, we have to expect more from ourselves and less from others. You are in control of your own LIFE and not the lives of others. Those who ignore you now will need you later, and those who don't want you when you're down don't deserve you when you're up.

In his heart a man plans his course, but the LORD determines his steps.

—Proverbs 16:9

APPRECIATE YOUR LIFE

This is your LIFE. Don't feed anger; don't provoke it or give in to it. LIFE is much bigger than beating yourself up and getting upset at what cannot be changed. Starve hate; starve negativity until it can't breathe any more. Be happy. There is much more to LIFE than offering negativity, hate, and other foolish, unwanted attitudes toward others and most importantly to ourselves. Enjoy what you have, because things do depreciate. I'm not going to lie to you; things will get dark, but don't let it stop you; you have to continuously be strong. Everything happens for a reason. If something happens to you and it's not according to your wishes, don't moan and groan; just adjust and move on. I know it's easier said than done, but good or bad, hit the reset button and start over tomorrow. And don't forget, pray for the best results. As the saying goes, Happy moment, praise God; difficult moment, seek God; painful moment, trust God; every moment, THANK GOD.

As Tony Gaskins said, *you can't keep carrying people and expect them to learn how to walk. If you're living to please others, then you'll always be lacking.*

Listen, we will all die; death is inevitable. The goal isn't to live forever. The goal is to create something that will forever live on in others. Be who you want to be, not what others want you to be. Cherish every moment that's given to you because it will not last a lifetime.

LIFE brings many problems, so instead of crying about them, pray and see how you can make things better. Things happen, good and bad. Learn to accept them, and stop complaining to others about your problems. Half the people don't care what you have to say, and the other half are happy that it's happening to you and not them. As I always say, to worry is to doubt God's abilities.

Who of you by worrying can add a single hour to his life?

—Jesus Christ

We need to make changes, not excuses. LIFE isn't about how hard you hit, it's about how hard you get hit and keep moving forward—how much you can take, and what you are capable of handling. That's called winning. Pain is only temporary; you have the right to be anything you want to be, and no one can tell you differently. *No one*! Be the best, because giving up is a coward's job. The things that happen to us don't shape our lives, but the way we deal with them is what makes us strong individuals.

LIFE is not about expecting, hoping, and wishing; it's about doing, being, and becoming. It's about the choices you have made and the ones you're going to make; it's about the things you choose to say. It's about what you're going to do after you finish reading this book. So remember, LIFE has many different chapters for us. One bad chapter doesn't mean it is the end of the book. Bad chapters are what we need in order to get to the end of the book successfully.

LIFE is not a relay race; we don't have the same starting point, nor do we finish at the same time. Just because someone else got somewhere before you doesn't mean you're too late. When will we realize that time stops for no one? Grow up, be willing to learn, be yourself, and leave a mark, because in ten years it won't matter what shoes you wore, what clothes you had, or how popular you were; all that will matter is how hard you worked and the impression you have left on the world.

LIFE is a test, the hardest test that anyone can ever take. There is no studying or knowing the next question, as though you were preparing for the SAT. Each question gets harder, but we must pass, we must push to the limit, and sometimes on faith alone. When LIFE gets hard, keep your head high, and remember that your everyday actions will affect you in the way you live your LIFE and the way you raise your family. If you love your family, you will sacrifice anything and everything to make them happy. It isn't just about you any more; it's about you and your family.

Love is a gift, not an obligation, because in LIFE, it has been said, sometimes you've got to run away so you can see who will run after you. Sometimes you've got to talk more quietly just to see who is listening. Sometimes you've got to step up in a fight just to see who's by your side. Sometimes you've got to make a wrong decision to see who's there to help you fix it, and sometimes you've got to let go of the one you love just to see if they love you enough to come back.

Christian pastor, author, and educator Charles R. Swindoll once said, "*The longer I live, the more I realize the impact of attitude on LIFE. Attitude to me, is more important than facts. It is more important than the past, education, money, circumstances, failure, success, and what other people think, say, or do. It is more important than appearance, giftedness, or skill. It will make or break a company, a church, or a home. We have a choice everyday regarding the attitude we will embrace for that day. We cannot change our past, or we cannot change the fact that people will act in a certain way. We cannot change the inevitable. The only thing we can do is play on the one string we have, and that is our attitude. I am convinced that LIFE is 10% of what happens to me and 90% of how I react to it. We are in charge of our attitudes.*" I love this quote and I believe your attitude mirrors your appearance on LIFE.

In my LIFE I wasn't always motivated or inspired to live a better LIFE. I changed because I wanted to be a positive role model for others. I have nine nieces and nephews, five girls and four boys, and they all look up to me. They love what I'm doing to encourage the youth and help students think more about the situations that are going on in their lives. I have dreams and goals just like everyone else; I fall, but I dust myself off and get back up; I cry, but I wipe my tears and move forward. What I'm trying to say is, when LIFE gets tough, we need to get tougher. We have to be positive role models for the next generation, and do what we have to do to set positive examples in our loved ones' lives. I remember days when I was very impatient and hungry, days when I wanted success now, and things weren't going my way at all. I thought LIFE hated me, but then I came to an understanding that success and great things don't happen over night; it's a process of hard work, determination, love, and commitment. We have to understand that things aren't always going to be what we want them to be. LIFE will treat you unfairly and will put shadows over your happiest days, but it's up to you to move on; it's up to you to say *I'm not going to let the bad days ruin my good LIFE.* I love my LIFE; I'm not perfect and I make mistakes, and the best thing about making mistakes in LIFE is that learning from those mistakes is what makes LIFE worth living.

God looks for steady growth, not instant perfection.

The most important thing to do is to enjoy LIFE and be happy; that's all that matters. Accept whatever comes in your LIFE; this will help you to enjoy LIFE even more. Learn to accept the bad and the good, and the rights and the wrongs, because self-motivation and acceptance is very important while enjoying LIFE. Enjoying jokes and being funny is very important in LIFE. If you can laugh, you can solve any problem that comes in LIFE. As the proverb says, *If you see a friend without a smile, give him one of yours.*

It is not only necessary that we focus on our enjoyment. It is also necessary to make the people around us happy; we can benefit their lives just by being in them. Sharing our enjoyment and happiness is a great thing. Even singing songs will free your mind from all distractions—and believe it or not there is always a song that will fit your feelings. Singing creates happiness inside you and makes you tension free. Be grateful for what you have, more than anything else; being abundant is about how you see LIFE. Some people may have everything, but they still feel poor. Others may have less, but they feel abundant. You need to look at what you already have and be grateful for it instead of complaining and yearning for things you don't have. Some people need to go through a painful loss before they can appreciate what they have. Doing what you love is the cornerstone of having abundance in your LIFE. Never forget that LIFE is precious. Live LIFE to the fullest while appreciating every moment, and put your whole heart into everything you do.

Don't let LIFE make you look weak. Be like a duck! Looking cool, but paddling like hell underneath.

—Reverend Run

Ashley Smith, a successful author and speaker, said, *LIFE is full of beauty. Notice it. Notice the bumblebee, the small child, and the smiling faces. Smell the rain, and feel the wind. Live your LIFE to the fullest potential, and fight for your dreams.* Smith understands the meaning of LIFE. There is so much more to LIFE than we can ever imagine. In LIFE, to love is to risk not being loved in return. To hope is to risk pain. To try is to risk failure, but risks must be taken because the greatest hazard in LIFE is to risk nothing. You can't buy love, but you can pay heavily for it. Love is a lot like a backache; it doesn't show up on X-rays, but you know it's there. You can't put a price tag on love, but you can on all its accessories. What the world really needs is more love and less paperwork. The purpose of LIFE is to live a LIFE of purpose. My LIFE has been filled with love, happiness, and fortune. I'm rich because I can count all the priceless things in my LIFE that money can't buy. The personal LIFE deeply lived always expands into truths beyond itself. LIFE is partly what we make it and partly what it is made by the friends we choose and the people we hang out with. We can do great things on this earth with great love, because without love, LIFE is empty.

This is your LIFE and you do not need anyone telling you how you should enjoy it or that you should appreciate it more. You are in that phase of your LIFE where you know what you want, but not necessarily how to get it. And this is what you are going to figure out. Your thoughts are lengthy, as they are in fact the direct interpretation of your ambition and your dreams. We are not promised a tomorrow, but tomorrow is what we hold in hope, without hope for tomorrow there is no future. Live for today, hope for a better day tomorrow, and plan to live a long and happy LIFE.

Appreciate LIFE as you are, appreciate and admire love. This is one certain way to fulfill ambition, to have LIFE doubled, joy multiplied; to have no regrets; to have it now and forever. Often, when we have what we're happy with, we push for that a little bit more; sometimes it becomes unbearable for our partner, who ends up falling out of love with you. You then realize that you were happy with what you had, and that wanting that little bit more can eventually push others away, and we end up alone, back at the beginning, swearing to never do it again. But LIFE has a funny way of repeating itself. Sometimes we can break this habit and, Lord knows, most of us try. Those who cannot are the ones who never settle, who wonder why they are by themselves and why LIFE suddenly seems like such a lonely place. As the saying goes, *You don't know what you have until it's gone*, and that's because we take things for granted because we do not appreciate them. LIFE is short, so live each day as if it's your last.

FIVE STEPS TO A BETTER CONNECTION WITH YOURSELF

#1 A NEW DAY

Making simple, conscious decisions about your everyday LIFE can influence your physical and mental well-being. Following through on the right resolutions about your health and lifestyle choices is not difficult, especially if you have a firm idea of areas you want to improve, and understand that small, gradual steps typically have better results than cold-turkey or all-or-nothing approaches. Take some time today to consider areas of your LIFE you would like to improve. You may want to be healthier, more generous, less stressed, or just more optimistic. Once you determine your goals, create a timeline and attach some simple steps. Consider your strengths and how they can help you on your path, as well as your weaknesses and ways you can work around and with them. If, during your progress, you take a step backward, keep looking forward. Most goals are reached with both good and bad days playing a part!

#2 CELEBRATING FRIENDS AND FAMILY

When it comes down to it, friends, family, loved ones and acquaintances who make you feel more alive, happier, and more optimistic are some of the most important treasures in LIFE. All the money and power you can imagine are not likely to be as satisfying as good conversation, trust, dependability, and laughter. Today take a moment to think about the special people in your LIFE, and ways you can keep those relationships strong. Make it a priority to spend some time each week with at least one of them - whether by phone, e-mail, in person, or through a letter. Human connectedness is a powerful healer, one we should all share in.

#3 Learning to Forgive

Forgiveness is beneficial not only mentally but physically as well. People who forgive tend to be less angry, depressed, stressed out and anxious, and have lower blood pressure and heart rates than those who hold grudges. If you tend to have a hard time letting go of a grievance, consider that forgiveness does not mean you have to forget an incident, but rather that you can place a limit on how it affects you and your relationship with another, and that you benefit from the process as much as the person you have the grudge with.

#4 Reconnecting with Yourself

Multiple commitments and hectic schedules can cause upsets to your daily LIFE. To stay balanced, relaxed, and calm, it's necessary every so often to regroup and decompress. Read a book, start an art project, work in the garden, or treat yourself to a massage.

If you find that the demands on your time are overwhelming, don't be afraid to politely say "no" when someone asks you to do something. Learn your limits. You can't do it all and you shouldn't feel guilty about it. Be a little selfish once in a while by scheduling "me time"—it will help keep you in touch with yourself in the year ahead.

#5 Rejuvenate Your Spirits

Been feeling stressed out after watching or reading the news lately? Then you need a "news fast"—avoiding news on the television, newspaper or the Internet for a few days or even a week—may help renew your spirits. It is a good way to gauge how you react to and process news, and how the news affects you.

Before I end this chapter on Love and LIFE, I will answer a question that someone once asked me and that I made a promise to answer. They asked, *What's more important, money or love?* Here is my answer. Money is a necessity to live LIFE; love is not. While love is wonderful, a feeling like no other, it doesn't put food in your belly or shelter over your head. In LIFE, both money and love are very desirable, but money is the one our society requires us to have in order to get by. However, I believe that love is most important. Money can be acquired through effort, but money doesn't amount to anything without love in your LIFE. Money can buy you things, but love can support you in spiritual, mental, and emotional areas of your LIFE. You can have all the money in the world but you truly aren't happy if you don't have love. Yes, money is important, but love is more important; love is the reason you and I exist. While I value love more than money, that is not to say I don't value money. But I care about money only to the extent that it allows me to live a relatively comfortable LIFE. I believe that when I'm on my deathbed looking back on my LIFE, I will feel complete knowing that I have lived a LIFE full of love, a LIFE that was more satisfying than a LIFE spent pursuing money.

2

INSECURITIES

The things you want are always possible; it is just that the way to get them is not always apparent. The only real obstacle in your path to a fulfilling life is you, and that can be a considerable obstacle because you carry the baggage of insecurities and past experience.

—Les Brown, Motivational speaker

I'm a truth speaker. I'm going to tell the truth and nothing but the truth throughout this entire book. I don't like my height at all. I seriously detest my five-foot-six-inch stance in every way. When I was younger I was very insecure about my height, especially amongst my tall friends. I was one of the shortest kids in my elementary school, in my junior high school, and I'm not sure but I think my high school, too. However, I was also a handsome, dark-skinned young man with the confidence of an army.

My height didn't stop me from playing basketball or football, running track, or even trying out for the wrestling team. I had healthy self-esteem and felt confident about anything I tried to do. My insecurity about my height never hindered my progress or my desire to succeed. Where my security left off, my ambition and self-esteem took over. I wanted to go to the NBA at one point in my LIFE. I knew I was short. I knew I wasn't tall enough to grab the rim. That didn't stop me from still trying to be the best basketball player in the world; it was my confidence and my ambition that empowered me to ignore my insecurities.

There were occasions when I prayed to God to grow a couple of inches, but instead I've grown to be more comfortable with who I really am. I realize that I am much more than a short guy or a nice-looking man. The purposes I have to fulfill and the goals I hope to achieve have no physical appearance or height requirements.

Never give your insecurities a voice or allow them to speak for you. This wisdom comes from recognizing that envy is a silent killer. Instead of envying what others have, begin counting the blessings, talents, and skills you possess. Be happy for others when they succeed and achieve great things in their lives. Your happiness about their successes shows that you can handle your own success someday. Besides, why make an enemy of people who could possibly impart something of value to you? Befriend those who are pursuing their goals; don't allow envy to rob you of an opportunity to grow and learn. For growth and the ability to learn will be integral to your own success.

Personal Application

In February of 2011 I didn't leave my house for two weeks because I felt as if I was gaining weight, and I didn't like the way I looked. I felt that my face was getting fat, my thighs were big, and my stomach wouldn't go down. As much I was going to the gym, I wasn't seeing any results. I felt sick. I was in bed most of the time, eating snacks, drinking soda, and watching TV. I was so unmotivated. I looked in the mirror and before I knew it, things became worse. My nose looked huge. My chin looked long. My eyes looked as if they were too close together, and I realized I had no ear lobes. I was pissed off at my appearance. I didn't want to talk to anyone—just eat, sleep, and dwell on my perceived imperfections. I hated my weight and the way I looked. Do you see how our thoughts can take us on a rollercoaster ride? We must stop them before they even get started.

I share motivational and inspirational thoughts on Facebook and Twitter regularly, but at that time, when I really needed to say or hear something uplifting, I couldn't. In the middle of the second week, I realized that giving advice to others is easier than applying that advice to your own LIFE; we often don't like to judge or critique our own faults, but instead choose to just accept them. I realized that I am no different to anyone else and that no one in this world is perfect. I jumped out of bed and said aloud with pride, "My insecurities are what give me strength and make me different; I feel secure in who I am." This is who I am.

Love me without fear. Trust me without questioning. Need me without demanding...Accept me without change, is valuable advice from best-selling author Dick Sutphen. Be the leader of your own LIFE. People can't affect you, lead you, or change you—unless you allow them to do so. You are stronger and smarter than ever. Insecurities may affect your LIFE, but insecurities can't control your LIFE unless you let them. Be free.

Dear anyone who has low self-esteem, you're absolutely beautiful.
Your smile is amazing, wear it more often. I love you.

—Keishorne Scott

CONTROL YOUR THOUGHTS AND INFLUENCE YOUR ACTIONS

I believe that insecurities are what hold most people back. Your mind is your greatest asset. Don't let anyone claim it. Once you allow someone into your head, you risk confusing your thoughts with that person's and can lose your own voice. Never allow anyone to make you feel "less than" yourself or anyone else. You are an amazingly beautiful and unique gift. Be yourself for yourself. Just as businesses perform analyses of their strengths, weaknesses, opportunities, and threats (SWOT) to help them grow or expand, it is essential that you take inventory of the company you keep and the thoughts you allow to settle in your head. The problem and the irony of insecurities is not that other people talk behind your back or judge you but that you already had the negative thought in your mind to begin with. Change the way you think and you can accomplish a lot. Be happy with whom you are, and consider the unique role that you can fulfill. Ponder these thoughts instead of the defeating ones that hold up a magnifying glass to your faults.

Not only do we need to change—the people like me who were once insecure and those who still are—but everyone who plays a major role in our lives needs to change, as well. Insecurity is directly tied to individuals' self esteem. If they think that they are horrible and a problem to society, then they will eventually become that. But if people think positively, they will influence their actions positively. LIFE-giving thoughts about yourself and the person God created you to be will enable you to use your gifts, talents, and skills in a positive manner that benefits society. Always remember that our actions are the direct result of the thoughts in our heads. Negative thoughts equal negative actions and reactions. Consider that it only takes a few negative actions in society for us to be labeled a burden instead of a contributor.

DEALING WITH OTHERS

Don't neglect or ignore those who care for you in an attempt to earn the approval of those who don't. Living to please others will certainly leave you feeling insecure when the reality is that you have no reason to be. Don't busy yourself looking for faults within yourself or others while overlooking the good. Your talents are unique and your flaws make you human. Invest in relationships that echo this fact and surround yourself with people who are beneficial and uplifting to you. Ultimately, we all must accept that LIFE is not perfect and neither are we. Mistakes will be made. People will cry. But things will get better in just a matter of time. Time rarely fails to put things in their proper perspective.

Personally, I do not allow people to bring me down with their words or actions; neither do I allow my insecurities to speak for me anymore. I am stronger than that, and I refuse to be a victim of other people's negative emotions or actions. Similar to a cover-up, they hope to disguise how they truly feel about themselves. Maybe they had a poor childhood or something else caused them to be sad and lonely. Don't judge them. You can't understand their feelings because you have not walked their path. We all have to learn this concept. Why waste time and energy on other people's misconceptions of you? We cannot allow our fear, anger, or self-doubt to be fed by other people's perceptions of us. This is a distraction that can deter us from achieving our goals and realizing true happiness. What we see in others is often a reflection of ourselves. This is why insecure people focus on the obstacles and confident individuals overcome them. Perception is the key to understanding yourself and how others view you.

People with confidence spend their time building up other people and helping them realize their own potential. I believe that as long as you are confident within yourself, it doesn't matter what anyone else believes. You can get what you want out of LIFE. Ignore and stay away from people who tell you otherwise. Brush them off. Keep them off. Leave them off. None of us need that kind of negative energy around us while we're trying to succeed. Surround yourself with people who share your ambitions and beliefs. Don't work hard to be belittled by the negative few; keep the love and company of the positive many.

THE TRUTH

Always do what you want, and say what you feel, because those who mind don't matter, and those who matter don't mind is a famous quote from children's book author Theodor Seuss Geisel, better known as Dr. Seuss. Perhaps there is a lesson to be learned here, that we should teach our children to be free of insecurities by embracing who they are from the beginning. If their interests, hobbies, or goals differ from those of their friends, we must encourage our children to pursue them anyway.

I was never the type of person to judge others, for many reasons. We don't really know people; we only know what they allow us to know. We don't know what has shaped them inside and out or what their experiences have been. So, never allow anyone to convince you that you're not good enough; we all are good enough. We all have a purpose in LIFE to be great; we only need to encourage and uplift one another. In the words of Marianne Williamson:

Our deepest fear is not that we are inadequate. Our deepest fear is that we are powerful beyond measure. It is our light, not our darkness that most frightens us. We ask ourselves, who am I to be brilliant, gorgeous, talented, and fabulous? Actually, who are you not to be? You are a child of God. Your playing small does not serve the world. There is nothing enlightened about shrinking so that other people won't feel insecure around you. We are all meant to shine, as children do. We were born to make manifest the glory of God that is within us. It's not just in some of us; it's in everyone. And as we let our own light shine, we unconsciously give other people permission to do the same. As we are liberated from our own fear, our presence automatically liberates others.

I will reiterate that you are a gift; you are amazing, and you are beautiful. Be you and no one else. I'll keep saying that until it seeps into your heart. It is the truth. We shouldn't feel insecure because we are overweight, too skinny, too short, too tall, shy, or any other things you can feel insecure about. Love yourself and be kind to yourself and others. Accept that God made you as the man or woman you are. This does not mean you don't work on areas that make you feel insecure, but you don't allow anything about yourself to be a reason for thinking less of yourself. Think about it. Did you have any control over your looks, familial ties, or the situation you were born into? No one does. Take what you have and make it something worthwhile. Your past does not have to be an indication of your future.

When it seems like nobody cares, God cares. When it seems like nobody is there for you, God is ready to listen.

HAVE STANDARDS

People often overlook the damaging effects that bad company can have on their self-esteem; it can actually cause them to develop new insecurities. Don't allow people to treat you just any kind of way. Playing the fool won't make you a better or more popular person but it will negatively affect your self-image and self-esteem. Have standards for the types of people you allow to gain access to your LIFE. When you allow yourself to be mistreated, it affects your thoughts; knowing how thoughts fuel actions, it is just not wise to be around those who don't appreciate and love you.

The world already has enough carbon copies, people who are too afraid to make their own legacy so they choose to settle for what their parents, friends, or even enemies think they should be or should pursue in LIFE. Never try to become someone you're not, to impress people who do not matter. It is truly that simple. There comes a time when you have to stand up and shout: "*This is me*! Accept me or reject me. This is my LIFE, not yours. Keep your judgments to yourself. I will be just fine."

HOW TO OVERCOME

Refusing to allow negative people to influence you is one thing. But you still have to deal with the things that make you feel insecure. How do you do that? You need to expose yourself to activities that involve your insecurities. If body image is a problem, go somewhere the public gathers to participate in group activities. Watch and observe people of all sizes enjoying themselves. Greatness has no shape or size, complexion or face. Greatness is within you. Shape, size, complexion, likes, or skills have no bearing on your ability to enjoy LIFE. If you are self-conscious about anything, make that the focus of your observations. Make an effort to address your insecurity instead of feeding it. Find something that you are good at and fully participate in it, so that you allow yourself to be involved with other people who also acknowledge it as an area of insecurity in their lives. In time you will come to the realization that we are all different but what matters in this LIFE is being happy, being useful to others, and giving and receiving love. No matter what you feel insecure about, those feelings can be overcome. They are only as much of a hindrance as you allow them to be. We all have gifts and abilities. Learn to appreciate the gifts you possess, and focus on the unique traits that make you an individual. You were given your unique gifts to play a unique role. Find out what that role is and play your position.

Realize that people really aren't watching you twenty-four/seven as you think. Those times you tripped over a crack in the sidewalk or slipped on the ice—quite often others didn't even notice or weren't paying attention. Even if they did, why should you care? Who has not tripped, fallen, or made a mistake? Be confident in who you are, no matter what anyone else thinks. Remember that the way people treat you is their karma; how you react is yours. Additionally, don't fool yourself into thinking that having material things will eliminate your insecurities. These temporary fixes only bandage the sore. Delve deeper to acknowledge and face the insecurities. What happens when your material items lose their value? What now? Material things will never keep you from feeling miserable about yourself. Food for thought: if you want to feel rich, count the things you have that money can't buy.

Value your assets that don't have a monetary value. A lot of us are blind, ignorant, and lost, thinking material items are what should motivate us and define our standards. There's nothing wrong in wanting to have nice things, but going into debt to impress others should be a felony. Work hard and the nice things will come. Working hard to acquire them will help you understand their true value instead of placing your value in them.

FOUR STEPS TO A BETTER YOU

I believe that there are four steps in becoming more secure and confident with yourself and the beautiful individual that you are.

Step #1: The first step in becoming more confident is to accept and love yourself.

You should make a list of all your positive traits and strengths on a piece of paper or in your journal. By doing this, you are reminding yourself that you too have praise-worthy qualities like others. You will see the value in yourself and your contributions to those around you.

Step #2: The second step is to motivate yourself.

Tell yourself that you can do it. Say it aloud. Words are powerful. Motivate yourself each and every day by hanging around positive people who will guide you and keep you uplifted in your spirits. Don't waste time associating with the wrong crowd, because they will only feed your insecurities and keep your energy low. Staying motivated, inspired, uplifted, and encouraged is important to improving your self-image and self-esteem.

Step #3: The third step is to face your fears.

Some people always have a fear that they will never be successful in anything they do. Such insecurity will be a disadvantage and will only cause you to sabotage yourself. Get rid of this fear by reminding yourself that if you haven't tried something, then you can never succeed or fail. For example, if your boss is asking you to lead a team, but you fear that you will make a mess out of it, how can you effectively lead? Such a fear may prevent you from taking on that task at work but also prevent you from gaining the necessary experience to advance to a higher paying position. But if you were a confident person, you wouldn't think twice about failing and would gladly take on that task, almost certain of your success. Do you see how lack of confidence can affect many areas of your LIFE, including important areas such as your career?

Step #4: The final but equally important step is to accept failure.

When you miss the mark or make mistakes, don't spend too much time thinking about it. If you are always crying over the mistakes that you will inevitably make in your LIFE, you will never get anywhere. Always remember that past mistakes and failures cannot be reversed and what's done is done. Their value lies in your ability to turn mistakes into 'lessons learned.' Being a confident individual will require you to look past those failures in your LIFE, gather any wisdom you can, but ultimately keep moving. After all, failures are an integral part of becoming successful. Albert Einstein said it best: *Anyone who has never made a mistake has never tried anything new.*

MOVING ON

You should ask yourself what you actually gain from being insecure. People are never more insecure than when they become obsessed with their fears at the expense of their dreams. Nobody can make you feel inferior without your consent. It's not who you are that holds you back, it's who you think you're not. We have to learn to be our own best friend because we fall too easily into the trap of being our own worst enemy. We need to stop looking at others with a desire to be them. Move past this stage and discover what you can offer the world, your community, and your friends. Remember the power of your thoughts and their influence on your actions. This year make a conscious decision to grow beyond your insecurities, despite any other lurking fears inside you.

Don't let your greatness slip through your fingers because of fear and defeatist thinking. Consider yourself equal to others, and then you will not aspire to be someone else. You lack confidence because you do not understand that you are searching for something that is actually within you. Trust me, you will feel better when you acknowledge that others are no better than you. Another point to consider is that you are only seeing what they want you to, and you can be easily fooled into thinking that they are happier than you. Everything that glitters isn't gold. Recognize that making the most of what you have and staying focused on your talents is where you will grow and prosper. Be yourself and stay happy, confident, and friendly—even with your enemies.

Learn to be alone without feeling lonely. Survive with your own LIFE. Trust God, yourself, and few people. In the end it's not about who you wanted to be, but who you ended up being.

SETTING A NEW COURSE

To be honest, I'm making some significant changes in my LIFE, such as how I do things and whom I associate with. This is reality: either change or be changed. I don't need to associate myself with the wrong crowd, because I'm smarter than that, and I was raised to never blend but to always stand out. Let's keep it real; a lot of people out there don't want to see you do well. It's the outright truth that people who don't even know you will hate you and try to derail your dreams. Why? Because they are insecure and uncomfortable with themselves; they get their temporary energy by putting down others. I'm writing this to tell you that no one can walk over you unless you're lying down. Take responsibility for the role you play in your happiness or demise.

Many are afraid to be great because they don't want to be criticized by those who choose to be average. Instead of being envious, be inspired. Reverend Run once tweeted, *everybody wants to be on top, but at the top everybody takes shots…so be ready to catch or dodge rocks.* Food for thought: Haters don't actually hate you; they hate themselves, so they take it out on you.

Don't shrink in fear because of criticism.
The biggest critics only critique what they couldn't create.

YOU ARE NOT THE ONLY ONE

People who are insecure have a need to categorize and judge everything, including people, because it makes them feel less threatened. It's their way of saying "I'm just as bad as you are, but I prefer to let everyone else know by judging you publicly." We should never judge a book by its cover, because we never know what someone went through or what he or she is going through. Honestly, that is why I sometimes isolate myself from people. I am not afraid to take criticism, but I know how detrimental it can be to your esteem and image. It is just best to stay away from people who subject you to their obviously insecure behavior.

Remember to live your own LIFE and depend less on the attention of others. Be yourself, because imitation is suicide. When people imitate others they give up who they themselves are. Abandoning one's personality for a cheap imitation is like a suicide. Therefore: imitating someone is killing oneself. Reject what others think of you if it does not align with what you think of yourself or want for yourself. It's your LIFE. You decide who to include or block out. Never give this control to anyone else. Accept that everyone will not understand everything, because everything isn't for everyone. You can handle your insecurities if you pray to God and get comfortable with the fact that God created you the way you are for a purpose. It's an instant morale boost. Stop comparing yourself to others, and take LIFE as it comes. Remember your LIFE is a unique story; it is not borrowed, stolen, or inspired. It's supposed to be unique. Stop trying to control everything. Take everything in your stride, and get on with accomplishing your goals in LIFE. While many fail to execute plans because of their fear of failure, they also fail to see that only through experiencing failure will they be able to truly enjoy the fruits of success.

TAKE THE GOOD. LEAVE THE BAD BEHIND

There's always a lesson to be learned from insecurities and failures. I know exactly what it is like to feel insecure and down all the time. Positive attracts positive while negative attracts negative. What really helps me is to compliment other people freely and often. I always strive to do good things for people, regardless of today's society where everyone is so critical and judgmental. Move past this societal norm, realizing that LIFE is too short to play stupid little games with pathetic people. Starting today, live your LIFE for yourself and no one else. In the end, you're all by yourself, and you have to learn how to be secure in your own skin. It takes time and practice but I'm sure you'll get the hang of it. *Carpe Diem*, which means *seize the day* in Latin, is an important concept to follow daily.

Surround yourself with positive energy, and set a goal to get outside at least once a day to do something that you enjoy. Don't let people stress you or allow their games to mess with your head. Remember that no matter what you are facing, it will pass. Time is constantly in motion. You will get over this bump.

I'm in my mid twenties but I've been through a lot. I've had to make a conscious decision to change for the better, and you can too. Remember how insignificant things appear in retrospect, and remember that LIFE is too short to focus on negative things for too long. Everyone gets insecure at times, to varying degrees. In fact, it's often the people who make a big show of being confident and outgoing who are the most insecure. Some people just have a tendency to be more shy, socially anxious, or insecure. Personally, I believe that experiences like being criticized by your parents or being bullied or ignored at school play a major role. They can lead to self-doubt and insecurity. No one can avoid these experiences, but implementing some of the solutions in this chapter and taking steps on your own to feel better about yourself will be beneficial and LIFE changing.

Just Keeping It Real

I sometimes battle with low self-esteem and social anxiety. While it is not always possible to trace particular episodes of insecurity back to the roots, it helps to be aware of your thoughts. Learn to notice signs that your insecure thoughts are overwhelming you and keeping you from things, rather than leaving them to grow and get out of control. Being aware will not only help you deal with your insecurities but also make it easier to reflect on what caused the insecurity in the first place.

My personal formula for staying secure within myself involves socializing with people who motivate me and inspire me to be better—the type of people who love me and care enough to tell me the truth and support me 100 percent when I set out to accomplish something. There was a time when I felt miserable and could not figure out why, but it was obviously the company I kept. It took a long time to change my negative thinking habits and learn how to be patient with myself. I began to change when I changed the people I associated with. This experience taught me to steer clear of negative people in the first place. While you cannot steer clear of your parents, you can control your reactions to them. Learn to act, not react. Consciously choose your positive feelings. Search for the positives in all things bad and good. Eventually it becomes a habit.

> *Hard work and perseverance pays off. I like myself a whole lot more now and can't wait to jump out of bed to start my day each morning. I am much happier!*

If you focus on self-improvement, you will be astonished at how easy it is to attract people with similar attitudes. You may even be able to influence the negative people around you.

Be consistent. Positive people are happy, friendly people, and will be enjoyable and nurturing company. Work towards being like this. Negative people will always bring you down and just bring drama to your LIFE. Don't be like this. Don't talk or interact with them. Stay away, because if they are not helping you, they are slowly ruining you. And while you can never completely avoid negative people, you can control how you deal with them. Others sometimes think that happy people are more fortunate, or that they don't understand the troubles of people less fortunate. This is not true. Happy people simply control what they can, adjust their perception, and make a conscious decision every day to be happy.

Basic Rule: If you feel good after being around someone, he or she is a keeper. If you feel bad around someone, forget him or her. Whatever you do, don't give up happiness in order to be anyone's friend. I call these types of negative people "Emotional Vampires" because they feed off your energy and leave you drained. They don't want your friendship, and they could care less how you feel. Stay away from people like this. I have known them all my LIFE and most never change. A person's emotional state can be as infectious as a disease. You may feel you are helping the drowning man but you are only precipitating your own disaster. The unfortunate truth is that some people draw misfortune upon themselves. Don't let them also bring it upon you.

I find it easier to treat everyone the same, keep my distance, and let them prove or disprove that they are genuine, over time. Many people tend to dislike others who are happy or content with their lives. They use gossip as their only source of socializing, and they befriend others because of their ability to acquire gossip. What a waste of time, when they could be using that same time and energy to improve themselves. Set time limits with people. Those who are positive get more of your time. Those who are negative get less. As you notice who are more positive, give them more of your time. As you notice who are negative, stop making plans with them. Being a friend does not require being a twenty-four-hour-a-day counselor for someone else's problems. You have your own LIFE to live.

Final Thoughts

Insecurities not only have the propensity to make you into an envious person; they can also ruin your LIFE by constantly making you feel you have to change for others. In my opinion, an identity crisis is the real root of insecurity and envy. Once you know who you are, you won't allow anyone to tell you differently. Spend time investigating yourself instead of listening to what others say about you. What a difference this shift in thinking and action can make in your LIFE!

Fear is another negative emotion that goes along with insecure feelings. Take a deep breath and just do it—execute in spite of fear. Don't limit your abilities because of your fear. Keep yourself always moving forward, and eventually you will overcome your fears and insecurities. Don't give yourself any other option than progress. It is true, not everyone will be able to completely conquer their fears or insecurities, but that should not stop you from pressing forward with your head held high. You are the only person who can facilitate change in your LIFE. The same applies to accomplishing your goals. Set a goal to face and conquer your fears. You can do it.

To improve your confidence, pick something you love about yourself that has been a positive contribution to someone's LIFE, and expand from there. If your patient listening ability makes you the best confidante, do it more often. Do you tutor well or lead others effectively? The point is to focus on your strengths rather than those things that make you feel insecure.

You have greatness within you. Share it with the world. Also important for increasing your confidence is asking yourself if your insecurities are reasonable. If they are, then try to find a solution; for instance, your weight can be changed. If, however, you find that your insecurities are unreasonable, ignore them. If something cannot be changed (a disability, or your family, for instance), then it must simply be accepted. The sooner you come to this conclusion, the better. Remember always to live off what LIFE gives you, not what it takes away.

A person who is humble is confident and wise.
He who brags is insecure and lacking.

—Lisa Edmondson, Actress

3

FRIENDS

True friends stab you in the front.

—Oscar Wilde, Irish writer and poet

Before I get into this chapter let me explain the quote, of Irish writer and poet Oscar Wilde. *True friends stab you in the front.* We don't have to take it literally. It means that true friends never mask what they feel and never hide anything that is for your own good, even if it hurts you in the process. True friends don't talk about you behind your back, nor do they try and sabotage your LIFE; if they do that, then they are not true friends. True friends are able to discuss things with you and be honest with you, rather than going behind your back. Only true friends can bring up touchy subjects and be brutally honest (yet kind) with you. It's a form of honesty, concern, and above all *love*!

I grew up in Brooklyn, New York, and like others, have mistakenly called people my friends who never were. When I had problems and needed their support, many of them vanished. That was when I first learned to be careful and to pay close attention to those I labeled as friends. We can't walk around with a crowd of envious people and expect them to be friends all of a sudden. They are who they are, and most don't even try to hide who they are. Don't be so needy that you ignore the signs your so-called friends show you. You could be entertaining an enemy. Reverend Run once said, *There are three types of people to stay away from in this world…the unexcited, the uninspired, and the ungrateful.* These are common characteristics among the snakes in your circle. Make sure none of your "friends" fit in these categories.

Learn to identify and appreciate your real friends. Set standards, and never demand what you are not willing to give. What is a friend? A friend is someone who understands your past, believes in your future, and accepts you just the way you are without reservation or conditions. Real friends will stand by your side when others desert you. They don't avoid you when you run into trouble. Real friends will never encourage you to do something stupid or dangerous. When you're in need, they will be there without question. They won't talk about you behind your back, but they will definitely defend you when necessary. They will stand by you whether you have money or not, and they truly want what is best for you. They have your best interests at heart. When you find these people, keep them and know that you are blessed. We don't need a thousand friends to be happy. A few good friends are plenty as long as they accept us for who we are and believe in us. When you think about it, having even one good friend is far better than a crowd of fake ones.

Never hold on to anyone who doesn't want to be held on to or hinders your progress. These are not your friends.

Friend or Foe

I've learned two things in life. First thing, is that everyone is not your friend;
and second thing, is that everyone is not going to be your friend forever.

—Miss Rain King

When I was fifteen years old I got caught stealing clothes at Macy's in Kings Plaza in Brooklyn, New York, not far from where I lived in Canarsie. I was with a friend, and like many young kids who wanted to be accepted, I did things that would make me look cool and make me feel important or qualified to be "The Man" amongst my peers. My friend and I went into Macy's one day to shop, but didn't have enough money for what we wanted. My friend said to me, "Keishorne, you got a big jacket on and can hold a lot of clothes in there." I said, "What! You want me to steal?" He said, "Come on man, do it for the team, man, we friends." I said, "OK, cool," and started putting T-shirts, sweaters, socks, towels, and whatever small items of clothing I could fit into my North Face jacket. As I started walking toward the exit, a police officer tapped my shoulder, showed me his badge, and said "Come with me, please." I shook my head in embarrassment and walked to the back of Macy's, where there was a small jail cell that I had to stay in while they took a photo of me, took photos of the merchandise, and called my parents. I was ashamed of myself. My friend hadn't taken anything, so he walked right out with no problem, while I was left to suffer the consequences. I'm from Trinidad, and my biggest concern was my mother's reaction to all this. I was very scared. My mother had to pay more than three thousand dollars for the merchandise I had attempted to steal. When I got home that night "it was on", and I refuse to get into details, if you know what I mean. Let's just say it was a long, painful night! The next morning my "friend" called and asked if I had the clothes. I said, no, I got caught. He said he knew that but wanted to know if I had the sweater he'd told me to get. I hung up the phone and never spoke to him again.

I've seen people turn cold faster than the weather. Bundle up.

—♥ Kimberly Hudson

I'm going to give you some advice: watch your friends closely. A lot of them are phony. Evaluate those around you. There is a lot of animosity out there and negative energy from so-called friends who will try to bring you down when they see you doing well and progressing in LIFE, but you can't allow this to bother you or deter you from your goals. If they aren't helping you become a better person, then they are not friends but spectators. I always say, *Behind every successful friendship is tolerance.* If people can't tolerate your faults and appreciate your values, they are indeed just spectators. Be aware.

Choose wisely who you label as friends. Determine who are friends and who are foes. Invest your time in those who are worthy and leave behind those who are of no benefit to you—or you can try to guide the misguided. Remember that friends are worth more than gold because their value is beyond comprehension. They are the people who will say, "That outfit doesn't look too good; I think you should change," instead of saying, "You look fine," even though you look a hot mess. Friends will always be with you, no matter how crazy you act or look. They're the ones who aren't embarrassed to be around you and are there through thick and thin. Learn to recognize and appreciate real friends.

There is a dark side to all of this: some people only appear to be real friends when in fact they have selfish intentions. They are the opposite of your friend; they are actually your foes. Foes can become bored with their lives easily, and decide to try and disturb yours. Foes fail to see the value in their own lives and will attempt to bring you down. You must learn how to identify and handle them. If people would simply take the time to really get to know one another, they would neither idolize nor hate others. These behaviors are not conducive for a friendship. Furthermore, the label of friend is often applied too quickly, before the qualities of a true friend are even noticeable. Time is a test of friendship. As they saying goes, it's not about whom you've known the longest, but who has never left your side.

Fake friends are really foes who can blend in pretty well, but you can tell who they are immediately if you are paying attention. They may have self-esteem issues or identity crises that cause them to run away or disown you at a moment's notice. They can be jealous and unforgiving, rude and self-serving. Real friends are the complete opposite. They don't point out your flaws to others, to bring you down, or hold on to petty issues.

Here is a detailed description of the foes in your LIFE. Ask yourself if any of your friends fit these categories. Fake friends will use you, drain your energy, rarely reciprocate a good deed or favor, try to keep you down on their level, find it difficult to praise you for your true qualities, or even try to convince you to change so that they can feel better about themselves. Fake friends are envious of your good fortunes, resent your relationships with others, need you for their gain, and never really pay attention to what is important to you. They can be summed up as selfish. They don't really care about you. They only care about themselves. They smile in your face, but as soon as you walk away they are talking about you like a dog to whoever will listen. Tip: If your friends talk about their friends *to* you, they will also talk *about* you to their friends.

Lots of people want to ride with you in the limo, but what you want is someone who will take the bus with you when the limo breaks down.

—Oprah Winfrey

Choose friends whom you would consider family. Treasure them because they will walk in when the rest of the world walks out on you. Family is not always about whose blood runs through your veins but about whom you care about and who cares about you. I'm grateful that I have friends in my LIFE who truly love me for who I am and not for whom they want me to be. They are family. Never forget that family and friends make LIFE worth living, and that LIFE is too short not to make the best and the most of everything.

ADVERSITY

Adversity is one of many things that will expose your real friends. You really find out whom you can rely on when troubles, sickness, or misfortunes come your way. *A problem will definitely separate the sheep from the wolves.*

I spoke with one of my friends a few months ago, sharing that I was writing a book entitled L.I.F.E. She said, "Wow, what is it going to be about?" I explained to her what the acronym stood for: Love, Insecurities, Friends, and Envy. She stared at me for a while before she began to dispense priceless advice about what real friends are, which I will share with you:

Real friends are people that you trust with your secrets, your hopes, and your dreams. They are those people that you know would gladly swim the seven seas for you and you would not hesitate to do the same for them. Real friends know when to give and take. They would do anything in their power to prevent you from getting hurt or experiencing pain, but if by any chance you ever do, they're the first people you can call and can cry to, and never will you doubt their motives. You can laugh with them until you get stitches, and ten years down the road you can still remember the joke and still laugh about it.

They know your faults and are not afraid to tell you when you're wrong—even if it might hurt your feelings—to build you into a better person.

Wow! She hit the nail on the head. What a powerful definition. Adversity will surely come in your LIFE, but you will not have to face it alone if you have real friends. They not only feel your pain, but they also actively seek ways to help you bear it, move past it, and overcome it. They view adversity as an opportunity to come closer to you, not as a reason to run away.

Anyone you label a friend should recognize your worth, have your best interests at heart, and love you enough to tell you the truth, whether you want to hear it or not. Real friends try to be worthy of your friendship because they believe you deserve that. They respect your needs to be alone, have company, be sad, or rejoice. They will genuinely rally on your side and wish the best for you in all circumstances.

We can't live without friends, but we don't have to be friends with everyone. Be selective! And remember, the greatest thing in LIFE is finding someone who knows all your mistakes and weaknesses but still finds you completely amazing.

ARE YOU A REAL FRIEND?

A friendship can endure adversity and will last longer when both sides are eager to take on the responsibilities of being a true friend. I'm sure that if we are better friends, we will attract better friends. Sometimes assessing yourself is the first place to start when issues arise in your friendships. Real friends can have big disagreements and still remain friends; they agree to disagree. Doing so is a sign of maturity and respect. Your real friends will respect you enough to give their views in a respectful manner, but also feel free to express their opinions because you are their friend. And when not speaking the truth will cause greater hurt in your friends' lives, you must be willing to sacrifice your needs for theirs. That is real friendship. It is give and take. Real friends understand they cannot expect to gain your respect without offering you their own.

Real friends can and will improve our lives. They come in all shapes and sizes, from all ethnic backgrounds and walks of LIFE. They may be people you are not related to by birth, marriage, or any other legal ties that bind. What will bind you together are things that really matter: ambitions, beliefs, needs, desires, and love. There are several types of friends, including casual friends, close friends, best friends, mentoring friends, and everything in between. Real friends will know when to take on different roles to fulfill your needs at the time. They are sensitive to what you need and jump to action at the perfect time.

Real friends are a blessing as well as a channel through whom great emotional, spiritual, and sometimes even physical blessings may flow. They will cheer us up when we're sad or depressed, challenge us to move beyond our regular boundaries, and motivate us when we're ready to give in. They will provide for us when LIFE falls apart. Are you a real friend?

FRIENDSHIP LOVE

Friendship love is a love that is totally honest, open, and comfortable. You really only have this kind of bond with a few people. You might know a lot of people and be "friendly" with them in a group situation, but they are not the best friends I am talking about here. I have a theory that you cannot truly be best friends with a member of the opposite sex. Down the line, romance will always come up from one party or the other, and feelings will be misinterpreted and mistaken. When this happens, the friendship will change and possibly never be the same again.

SET THE BAR AND HAVE HIGH STANDARDS

How can we recognize potential friendship? Signs include a mutual desire for companionship and perhaps mutual interests of some sort. Beyond that, genuine friendship involves a shared sense of caring and concern, a desire to see one another grow and develop, and a hope for each other to succeed in every aspect of LIFE.

A real friendship involves action. Do something for someone else while expecting nothing in return. Share thoughts and feelings without fear of judgment or negative criticism. A real friendship involves relationship. Those mutual attributes mentioned above become the foundation in which recognition transpires into relationship. Many people say, "Oh, he's a good friend of mine," yet they never take time to spend time with that "good friend."

Friendship takes time. Good friends should not be measured only based on the time spent together but you should dedicate time to get to know one another, to build shared memories, and to invest in each other's growth. The time will not only sort out the friends from foes, but also help you develop into a better friend. Time allows you to see what areas your friend needs help in, where you can assist, and lend a helping hand. It also helps you understand their insecurities and areas you can help build. Time will test your friendships, exposing vulnerabilities and areas of strength.

Friendship requires trust. Trust is essential to true friendship. We all need someone with whom we can share our lives, thoughts, feelings, and frustrations. We need to be able to share our deepest secrets with someone without fear that those secrets will end up on Facebook the next day. Failing to be trustworthy with those intimate secrets can destroy a friendship in a hurry. Faithfulness and loyalty are a must. Without them, we often feel betrayed, left out, and lonely. Proverbs 18:19 in the New Living Translation Bible say, *It's harder to make amends with an offended friend than to capture a fortified city. Arguments separate friends like a gate locked with iron bars.* When we've offended a friend, whether by breaking trust or telling them the truth with love, we risk losing that friendship. We must guard the trust with all diligence. If we sometimes offend a friend without meaning to, God's Word offers a solution. It's called forgiveness. Encourage one another and forgive one another when there has been an offense. In a real friendship, there is no backbiting, no room for negative thoughts or turning away. Genuine friendship supports during times of struggle and can survive the greatest catastrophe. Be dependable and demonstrate unconditional love.

A real friend is someone that will do almost anything for you and be there when you need them most, though they must also allow you to solve some of your own problems. I say almost anything because a friend needs to also be bold enough to stop you from doing anything stupid such as robbing a bank, hurting other people, or hurting yourself. The easiest example is cutting. As a lot of teens cut during this time and age, it is their friend's duty to stop them, not encourage it or brush it off. Friends will come when you call for help—anytime, anywhere, for any reason.

DIFFERENT TYPES OF FRIENDS

Friends are true assets in our lives if they are real. It *doesn't matter* what he or she looks like as long as they are responsible, reliable, and helpful. I think these people are the best people you can surround yourself with. There are different types of friends: coworkers, social workers, schoolmates, and more. Each type of friend is helpful in one way or another. Coworkers might help solve problems and relieve stress in the workplace, while friends from the community can widen one's perspective by connecting with people from different areas. Schoolmates can be encouraging when others try to belittle or bully you at school.

While it is very difficult to find a definition of a good friend that everyone will agree on, there are some common characteristics that most definitions share. The three main qualities that define a good friend are *loyalty*, *the ability to understand*, and *the willingness to give encouragement*. People with good friends usually have higher self-esteem, confidence in their abilities, and motivation in LIFE. Friends will encourage, inspire, and support each other.

FRIENDS WITH BENEFITS

Friends with benefits simply means friends who sleep together with no commitment or strings attached. This is very misleading and very damaging. First of all, this is not a friend; and second, there are few if any benefits. Sharing your body with someone is serious business and should never be entered into lightly. Friends with benefits break all the rules of true friends: they spend no time together outside of their "fooling around" and therefore have no real way to develop a friendship. Don't forget that these types of friends can also do sexual things with other people, likely exposing them to emotional scars and sexually transmitted diseases. Why would you subject yourself to this intentionally? This relationship usually does not end well.

Friends with benefits are not exclusive. Either party can become emotionally attached and take advantage of the other, who has no protection from harm. They do not have the trust and accountability that real friends have. If you are agreeing to this type of friendship because you hope it will evolve into a relationship, think again. If you like someone as a boyfriend/girlfriend, then make it clear from the beginning; otherwise you will end up having your heart broken and feeling used. Someone usually gets hurt in this type of friendship.

A lot of people, especially young men and women, are in no shape to have a friend with benefits. It is not healthy for the self-esteem or the body. It is just lust, not a real friendship at all. Be careful and guard your heart. Such an arrangement usually makes you feel more vulnerable and needy. It may seem innocent or insignificant, but it can have a damaging effect on your relationships and how you feel about yourself. Friends with benefits is essentially a girlfriend/boyfriend relationship that is open. Don't set yourself up for failure and heartache with this type of arrangement. You'll be way more attached and will find it harder to trust and love in real relationships. Plus, if word spreads that you are having casual sexual encounters you can get a very bad image in your community.

MENTOR FRIEND

My favorite type of friend is the mentor friend. Mentor friends are people you go to when you need advice. They always seem to know what you need to hear and when you need to hear it. They'll tell you the truth about what works in the real world; they speak the truth. They'll guide you because they've been there and done that. They have your best interests at heart and want you to avoid the trials and tribulations that they have endured, if you will listen to them. They have some things figured out and are more than happy to share their wisdom with you.

Everyone needs a mentor friend, and while he or she is usually older, wiser, and more experienced, age is irrelevant. Sometimes this friend is younger than you but able to understand things and pass along information in a positive way. This type of friend will build you and encourage you to be a better person. He or she will lift your spirits and encourage you to love yourself first.

Before you can love another person the right way, you have to love the person staring back at you in the mirror first.

I have a few mentor friends, and whenever I feel a little down or hurt they are right there to help me up and remind me that "everything will work out." I respect them because they speak the truth and bring me joy. Mentor friends won't demean you or look down on you. They give you words of wisdom, and then they help you implement those words to bring about positive results in your LIFE.

BEST FRIEND

Sometimes the true meaning of the term *best friend* is lost because it is so widely used. A best friend is hard to find, hard to let go, and hard to forget. A best friend goes above and beyond the call of duty, consistently. This person is your closest confidant and ally. He will always be there for you, won't judge you, and knows more about you than your other friends know. You can cry on her shoulder and know that she cares. She won't try to manipulate you or defame you. A best friend is someone you can depend on and trust completely with your whole heart because he has stood the test of time. He will see you through difficult times, encourage you in sad times, and rejoice with you in happy times. A lot of us need an extra push in LIFE, someone to motivate us and challenge us to be successful, great, and productive in LIFE. Your best friend is a person you love, someone who means a lot to you.

Your best friend is a very special person in your LIFE. He is the first person you think about when you make plans. She is the first person you go to when you need someone to talk to, and you can call her up just to talk about nothing—or the most important things in your LIFE. Your best friend gives the best hugs in the world! He shares your pain and your emotions. She would take a bullet for you if necessary.

Many people will have different best friends throughout LIFE. However, usually a person has only one real, true best friend in all that time. A best friend is not only someone you have a good time with but also someone you believe you can trust your LIFE with. A best friend is the first person you call when the most amazing things happen in your LIFE and when the most horrific calamities come your way. A best friend is the person you will always remember, no matter what circumstances or distances separate you.

A best friend is almost like real family, and her opinion counts the most with you. You can spend time with this person and very rarely grow tired of him. A best friend can show you gratitude. She will forgive you always, even when you've screwed up badly. A best friend transcends time and circumstances; she has a true portrait of who you are regardless of the time that has passed. A best friend is your comfort zone. You may have inside jokes that are only significant to the two of you. You know each other's family and may practically live at each other's house. You may call his parents Mom and Dad, and you feel safe sharing your secrets.

You will talk to your best friend on the phone in the bathroom, while you shower, and until you fall asleep. You love this person and all her faults, knowing that's what makes her who she is. You do many things together, and you don't need to worry about what he will think of you if you fall, cry, or make mistakes. He will act crazy with you and have no problem being silly with you. He might accidentally ruin your stuff or mess something up, but you just laugh because you love this person to death.

She always considers your feelings even though she teases you a lot. You say mean things to each other because you find it amusing. You two can laugh at random things that others would not understand. You genuinely love to be with one another and are probably very similar in personality and goals. This is the person you're not afraid to say, "I love you" to. You may have known him since kindergarten, or since high school, but the only thing that matters is that they are loyal.

Never tell a lie to make a friend, or to keep one.

—Tony Gaskins

FAMILY

There is no doubt that it is around the family and the home that all the greatest virtues, the most dominating virtues of human society, are created, strengthened and maintained.

—Winston Churchill

The word *family* is unique and special among different cultures and ethnic groups. It can be defined as any group of persons closely related by blood— such as parents, children, uncles, aunts, and cousins—or coresidents. I believe that those in your LIFE who do not fit this description should not be excluded. In my mind, a family is a group of people who support and help each other, with unconditional love. Regardless of sexual orientation or preference, all families embody these common principles. Family never leaves your side. Your family is much more than parents: it includes the people who are dear to you, who take care of you, and whose love for you exceeds boundaries or circumstances. People who fit this description are your real family.

Family does not kick you while you are down or take advantage when you're vulnerable. Family members will help without knowing all the details, but you don't mind sharing details because you don't feel judged or loved any less. Obviously, this definition does not necessarily include all of your natural family members, while it does includes those who have crossed your path and shown the utmost loyalty, respect, and love.

BREAKUP TO MAKEUP

I hated my mother! This was exactly how I felt a few years ago. One evening in December 2010, I got into an argument with my mother and said some very harsh words, which a son shouldn't even think of. I said, "You aren't my mother, and I'll hate you till death." I know, I know, I'm the worst son in the world, right? But I was very angry with her and the way she had made me feel throughout my life; it irritated me too much at times, and I didn't care what I was saying at that moment. Have you ever been so angry with your mom or dad that you just wanted to say whatever was on your mind out of anger? Because you just got so fed up?

Don't get me wrong, I love my mother with all my heart and admire her for her ambitious and hardworking qualities. She has often taken those extra pains to offer me a good life. But at times, her nagging attitude irritated me to no end. Let me tell you how it all got started. I had no job, no money, and no family support. I felt we hadn't ever been close, but things got even worse. We started having frequent fights. We yelled at each other more often than not, and a point came when I felt there was no love left. We began to display hatred for each other. Every day was an argument. Like my mother, I was too hardheaded, and that was perhaps one of the main reasons why we didn't get along well.

I decided to leave home after our big argument in December. I went to my friend's place in Queens and thought of staying there till things got settled. Initially, it turned out to be a great experience. I got a lot of time to relax, cool down, and recover my lost peace of mind. But after a while, things started changing I was now completely dependent on my friend for all my needs. I had to depend on him financially to meet up all my expenses. Soon it turned out to be lonely and frustrating without the family being around for the holidays. I was leading a life of a parasite. As the days passed, I started exploring myself. Since the argument with my mother, I had plenty of time to concentrate on my well-being. I began wondering what kind of person I was. I realized I needed to make some significant changes in myself. To be a better human being, I implemented certain self-evaluation exercises and started reading and writing whatever came to my mind. I began to understand that life hadn't been that bad to me. I realized that there were people in far worse states than I was in. I also realized I was committing a sin by not obeying one of God's most important commandments: "Honor thy mother and thy father."

I deeply regretted not respecting my parents and not giving them their due honors. I saw myself in the mirror and felt guilty for my acts. I realized my faults and repented for being stupid. I gathered all my strength and went home and apologized to my mother with all the guilt showing in my eyes. Being a mother, my mom forgave me, accepted my apology, and took me back in. After all this, I realized that I must respect my mother and my father, despite how they speak to me. No words can explain the relief I felt at that moment. I realized that there were better ways to respond to their yelling and complaining. By now I understand that my parents are like Gods in disguise. They are to be respected and obeyed and never to be disrespected. They are the ones who will never betray us and will accept us the way we are. So treasure the angels you have in your parents; if you give up one thing for them, they will give up a million more in return.

THE MOTHER OR MATRIARCHAL FIGURE

Your mother carried you in her womb and you looked to her for all your needs during the early part of your LIFE. Or you may have been adopted at a later stage or taken in by someone, but the mother's role was the same. She nurtured the good within you and lovingly helped you to move past detrimental or unhealthy habits, relationships, and responses. Others were raised by a grandmother, an aunt, or another maternal figure, who protected, sustained, and provided food and shelter—and all with love.

While not everyone experienced this type of relationship with their natural mother, everyone had someone who would dispense advice and provide guidance, just like a mother. Mothers can detect illness, sadness, or any other disruptive emotion in their children, even at a distance. Countless stories can be read about mothers. It is difficult to lie to a mother, even if she doesn't let you know that she knows you lied. Mothers often know things about you before you know them yourself. Many would call it a "sixth sense," but it comes naturally to mothers.

Mothers are not perfect. They make mistakes and do things that in retrospect they wish they had not done. Mothers also have to make unpopular decisions in the best interests of their children. They are bold and willing to withstand the frowns, tantrums, and silence. They can smell a rat a mile away, and they know your friends' motives. Teenagers often keep their friends away from their mothers out of fear of judgment, but fail to realize that their mothers can discern things that they themselves can't. A mother's experiences, her knowledge of relationships, and her wisdom should be seen as a benefit.

Increasingly, children are finding themselves in single-parent homes. The single mother, father, or guardian must play the role of both parents.

The Father or Patriarchal Figure

Fathers often play a very different role in their children's lives. Sometimes fathers are not as easy to talk to or even available to speak with. Fathers usually go to work, they spend less time at home, and they might maintain a more hands-off approach to parenting than the mom. Children look to them for security and protection, and they are their children's ultimate defender. Their love runs deep, whether they verbally express it often or not. Their actions of sacrifice, dedication to work or business, and providing a living are all selfless acts of love.

Fathers will teach you things you won't forget. Receiving practical information and sharing experiences with your dad can turn into beloved memories, whether it's changing the oil in your car, discussing how to tell if a boy really likes you, or attending a father-daughter dance.

Fathers can play a dual role: the enforcer and the "good parent." If your mother has to remind you about your chores too many times, or receives bad reports from school, she may involve your father. The father's word is final. Sometimes the very fact that he had to be involved is enough to ensure a stricter punishment than the one your mother would have given. As the "good parent," the father enjoys not having to nag you or correct every mistake you make at the dinner table or in general. Daughters especially have a way of getting the best out of their dads and can get away with a lot (except when it comes to boys).

Though fathers have an instinct to provide and protect, many kids are left with absentee dads, either because the fathers are working long hours or because they have given up. Having a family is a commitment and requires more than feelings and good intentions. Fathers are also known to share wisdom and provide a perspective that mothers cannot give in certain situations. It is a well-known saying and belief that "only a man can raise a man." One of the primary factors blamed for the breakdown of society is a fatherless home; some argue, however, that many successful, contributing individuals were raised in single-mother homes, making this an excuse instead of an explanation.

Like mothers, fathers are role models for behavior and relationships. A woman often will be attracted to men who are in some way similar to her father. Similarly, men often have similar behavioral traits as their fathers. How a man treats his wife can be similar to the way his father treated his mother. Children will usually imitate their parents even if they are told, "do as I say, not as I do"—a popular saying in our society. There are exceptions to every rule, but the fact remains that there are common characteristics, habits, professions, beliefs, and attitudes throughout families—immediate family members especially.

The role of a father can be demanding. However, the impact that being a good dad can have on the LIFE of the child—and the father himself—is satisfying. Many boys and adolescents with absent fathers have other men in their family or community who have stepped up to fulfill at least some of the responsibilities of the father.

Our parents teach us a lot just by being parents. Parents have the benefit of what they know, what they have been taught, and what they have seen their parents do. They implement things they agree with and leave out those they don't. Things do not always work out as they are planned. Decisions that parents make affect children, and children are not allowed to have an opinion. Family LIFE is designed this way on purpose, to protect you and provide you with guides who are more experienced than you are, for the world can be a peculiar place.

It is easy to blame external circumstances for our decisions and thought patterns. Our environments do affect us, but we are the final authority on every action we take. Even as young children, we decide which other children we like the most, who we want to play with, and who we want to be like. We decide what we like about them, and we decide to be their friends or playmates. We also decide which rules we will follow and which we will break. This pattern continues as we grow up.

It is important to identify this free choice that we have, even as children. Everyone is aware that the company we keep will influence our behaviors and thoughts. There is something within us that identifies with others and is attracted to them. This same something inside is what helps us decide whether we will follow the rules or break them. We decide whether the punishment would be something we could bear. The point is that while our parents have a great influence, we progressively gain more control over our own lives as time goes on. We can remember some of the things we knew at a young age, such as our thoughts and fears, things we were willing to try, and things we were afraid to try.

BROTHERS AND SISTERS

Sibling relationships can be protective, adversarial, envious, loving, patient, kind, unkind, and everything in between. Time and space would fail to explain all the things that go into our sibling relationships; however, we have to maintain a relationship with them, no matter how we may feel about them. There are those we love, and those who are more difficult to relate to. Usually, this type of relationship is unconditional, but it varies. Adult brothers and sisters might be close, or they might not speak at all. Their behavior can likely be traced back to the sibling relationships of childhood.

These relationships will also have to do with how well personalities get along. We can all think of things that we love and hate about our siblings. There may be some similarities between siblings, but most are very different. Children without siblings—"only children"—can have relationships with others that mirror a sibling relationship. The other scenario is an only child who is selfish and cannot relate well to others. Only children cannot be generalized; however, they do not have to "share" their parents with other children, so they receive more individual attention.

Whether we are the only child or we have siblings, we have other people in our lives who are similar to siblings. We may not have much in common with them, but there is deep love and loyalty. Some come in the form of best friends.

We may not feel entirely comfortable being ourselves with our natural siblings. Often we can relate better and be more transparent with strangers than we can with our family members, whose judgment we may fear.

Ideally, there is love, loyalty, respect, and unconditional support between the members of your family. Your grandparents, aunts, and uncles are all part of this network of support as well. They, too, have an influence in your LIFE, if they are an active part of it. Even in their physical absence, they can deposit ideals and behavior patterns that are apparent in later years.

Family members are the people who provide unconditional love and support. Despite disagreements or personality clashes, you can count on these people in all situations and every trial or tribulation in LIFE. They are the constant, the foundation on which society is built upon. The need for family can be understood by the differences we find within ourselves. Sometimes we need a father figure for a stern lecture that we may not want to hear at the time but know is for our benefit. Other times we need a hug, some kind words, and soup from our grandmothers or aunts. Depending on what is going on in our lives, someone in our family should be able to help and provide support.

FAMILY CONFLICT

It is inevitable that conflict will arise in familial relationships. Familiarity can indeed breed contempt. When it comes to elders and parents, respect is important. Respect the fact that they are here to guide, protect, and shield you from hurtful things. Respect them because God says so. Respect them so that you will receive respect. You will reap what you sow. Honor them.

Siblings should also be treated with respect. You should not treat your friends or a stranger better than you would your own sister or brother. Do not allow envy, sibling rivalry, or any other trivial thing to override the blood that binds you. If you have been hurt or mistreated, forgive—for your own sake. Holding on to past hurts and pains only burdens the person carrying them. Imagine being tied to a corpse that provides no help, only hurt. Don't allow yesterday to dictate today. Tomorrow is never promised.

How many conflicts within families are really worth the contention, division, and broken relationships they cause? When put into proper perspective, few things are worth severing family relationships for, yet this is all too common. There are legitimate reasons why it may be beneficial to discontinue communication with a family member. But most scenarios have more to do with conflicting opinions, miscommunication, and other fixable issues. It is sad when family members die, leaving others with regret or sadness for how things were before their passing. You have an opportunity to reflect on the issues that have caused you to cut off family members. Are they really worth it? If the family member died tomorrow, would you have any regrets? Family relationships help us get acquainted with the kinds of relationships we'll have later on in LIFE; there will be mothering, fathering, and sibling-type relationships—in your workplace, your church, your school, everywhere.

So what do you do when your boss corrects you about something and you want to go word for word? Count up the costs and make a decision. Arguing with your boss could cost you your job and reputation. Instead, you could use your experience of honoring and respecting your mother and father and apply it to this situation by honoring your boss. Knowing that this is for your own benefit, it should not be difficult to overlook how uncomfortable you feel at being corrected.

Any conflict within the family should be weighed against the value of the relationship. Is it so difficult, when you are right, to have been wronged, and misunderstood? When should one take the high road and perhaps overlook things because it is the mature thing to do? What about the definition of love in 1 Corinthians 13:5 that says, *love doesn't keep track of wrongs*? Ask yourself if you are too willing to sacrifice relationships for issues that really don't matter.

FAMILY BETRAYAL

One of the most infamous stories of betrayal involves Jesus Christ and his disciple, Judas Iscariot. Judas was not a blood relative of Jesus, but they traveled, taught, and lived together during Christ's ministry. He knew Christ's habits, thinking rationale, and behaviors even better than some of Jesus's own relatives did. These facts are what made the betrayal so hurtful. It was no stranger who led Jesus' accusers to Him, but a close friend—someone who knew Him well enough to cause Him pain. Betrayal is painful on any level. But betrayal by a family member or someone close can make you feel foolish, vulnerable, and naïve.

Children have been betrayed by parents, and vice versa. Siblings may stab you in the back for selfish motives, and close friends may prove to be your worst enemies. These people have all made a decision that their actions or words were more important than your feelings, needs, or desires. Do not worry. It hurts; it leaves a scar; it definitely will not be forgotten. The good news is that pain causes growth and scars form tougher skin.

Every experience in LIFE can be seen as either a learning experience or an opportunity to whine. Learning experiences have nothing to do with what we deserve or feel. They are good and bad experiences that shape us and provide wisdom that we can use in future experiences or to help other people in similar situations.

Family betrayal can also include molestation, incest, or other trust-violating behavior. It can have lasting effects on the child or adolescent victim. It can distort relationships and confuse boundaries that agree with societal norms. *Any type of behavior or action that makes you feel uncomfortable or question if it is right is likely a violation of what is acceptable.* Instinctively you will know when someone has crossed a boundary with you. It is not your fault, and I encourage you to confide in someone you trust. Sometimes all you can do is remove yourself. Do not feel alone or at fault; many children experience the same type of betrayal, unfortunately.

Family judges you, friends' talk about you, and people that you don't know will doubt you. And LIFE is still precious. I believe family isn't about whose blood you have, but who never leaves your side. Remember: let no one control your destiny! The pen that writes your LIFE story must be held in your own hand!

As you can see, family is supposed to represent a pillar of stone that we can always count on. When everybody else has turned their back on us, family remains. Even when our natural family fails to uphold moral values, most likely we can look to someone as a source of comfort and strength in our lives. If this is not the case, God is always near. We can call upon God at any time, in any circumstance. It is not a guarantee of understanding, but He will help us for sure.

Family and friends help make LIFE more enjoyable. We are not alone in our sadness or pain. We find common interests with our friends and we can share in happy and joyful moments with them as well.

A friend is one of the nicest things you can have, and one of the best things you can be.

—Douglas Pagels, author and editor

Below is a national resource you can use to get counseling, find answers, and get the help you need:

RAINN website: http://www.rainn.org/get-help/national-sexual-assault-hotline, phone #: 1-800-656-HOPE (4673)

Me (*left*), my mother (*middle*), my niece (*right*), my nephew (*in front of me*) and my little niece (Jahshana Olivierre) and nephew (Jahkeeda Olivierre) (*in the very front*)

I LOVE MY MOM.

My ravishing sister (Janice Olivierre) and me at my nephew (Jahdane Olivierre) baby shower. Our smiles are identical.

Me with my ravishing sister (*left*) and my beauteous niece (*right*) at the Shades of Beauty Fashion Event for Women's History Month. Told you our smiles are identical.

My handsome nephew (Jahdane Olivierre), the beauteous Jennisha Hosam, and me.

My prestigious friend Frantz Debrosse
Jr. and me at the Michaela Radio Show.

The stunning Kimberly Hudson
and me at The Millionaire
Brotherhood Success Seminar.

The Remarkable Jahshana Olivierre
(my niece) and me posing for the
camera. Family ♥.

The love of my life and a blessing from Heaven. My heart, my soul, my mother (Joyce Scott).

My Mother and my Father (Clyde Scott).

4

ENVY

"Envy eats nothing but its own heart."

—German Proverb

Envy is an unfortunate yet common emotion that almost everyone has or will encounter at one point in his or her life, often in response to feeling inferior. However, feeling this emotion at one point is not the same as being an envious person. To be an envious person means that you totally embrace this emotion, allow it to control your actions, and ultimately decide it is the proper response to your insecurity within. In general, envious people have an ungrateful and "woe is me" attitude towards God and society.

ENVIOUS ME

Growing up in Canarsie, I had many friends, but I had a main group with whom I spent most of my time with. My best friends were Nigel, Nyron, Chris, Carlos, and Richard. We called Richard "Dread," and no, he didn't have dreads, and to this day I do not know why we even called him that. Nigel was the center of everyone's friendship; we went to his house every day to eat, play, chill, and just do boy stuff that involved a lot of getting into trouble. Our crazy activities were the highlight of our friendship, and basketball was too, which we played almost every day of our life at one point. Nigel had been my best friend since third grade, one of the first friends I made when I first moved to Canarsie in 1996, and man did I love his family and his life. At times, I wished I were Nigel. As a matter fact, I wished it almost all the time. He had a nice home, a nice caring mother, a little sister who was beautiful, a dog, all the video game systems a kid could want, his own room, and everything else a young boy would want as he grew up.

I envied his lifestyle, from his family to his quality of living. Nigel wasn't necessarily spoiled, but he got almost everything he ever wanted. I was jealous and I envied him, because I had to work for what I got, while his family supported and provided for him as he was growing up. While I was working at Burger King, making next to nothing, he didn't work and still got everything he ever wanted. His mother was cool and one of the greatest women I had ever met, and to this day, she still is. I loved her a great deal, and his grandmother was truly God's gift to humanity. Her heart was divine. Nigel's lifestyle excited me, and I wanted it. And I'd even take his dog candy. But as I grew older, I grew out of my envious state of mind and learned to work hard for what I wanted and appreciate what I had. I realized that, even if my mother couldn't afford all that Nigel's family could, I still had a roof over my head, food on the table, and a warm couch to sleep on when I got home. I didn't get my first bed until I was about twenty-two years old. But I'm still grateful. I learned that I must be content with what God had given me. As the popular quote goes, we don't know what we have until it's gone.

Never envy what someone else has because you have no clue of what they had to endure to get it.

—Tony Gaskins

ENVY IS IGNORANCE, IMITATION IS SUICIDE

To be envious, one must discount or completely ignore their individual gifts and abilities. It implies that God has unfairly distributed talents and has given someone something that was not given to others. While no two people are gifted in the same areas, every person is gifted in some way. Envy can blind people, causing them to focus on others' gifts instead developing their own. In this chapter, I will discuss the importance of identifying envy and how to completely rid yourself of it when you see it springing up inside of you.

It's sad but true that people who don't even know you will envy you, while those who do will envy you even more. This can breed silent enemies among friends, family members, and associates. They are not always easy to identify, either because most have two faces: one they show you and another they use to talk about you. They will smile to your face and talk behind your back. They will pose as a friend to gain information about you and your aspirations, only to have something to talk about. They rarely have anything positive to say about others and can always see the negative side to any story. No matter how wonderful the news is, they have the ability to zero in on all the negative facts, even if there seems to be none. Expression of support and joy for your accomplishments is rare and difficult for them as they secretly wish you would fail.

They may be the "friend" that is willing to lend an ear whenever there is something bad happening in your life, but they become busy when you are sharing great news. They have little if any good intentions in their relationship with you and only stick around hoping to see the day when you fail. They have allowed this emotion to consume them instead of ridding themselves of it as soon as they see it.

COUNT YOUR BLESSINGS

A lot of people are jealous of others rather than inspired because they are secretly afraid that they lack the ability to do what they see others do. Most people never consider the fact that they have their own unique talents and should not aspire to do what others are doing. Be the head, not the tail. Be an original instead of a copycat.

Envy is the art of counting the other fellow's blessings instead of your own.

— Harold Coffin

Envy typically involves two people, and jealousy typically involves three people. It is very possible to feel envious towards more than one individual at any given time, though. Usually, envy involves desiring the beauty, wealth, or socioeconomic status of another individual. They stem from different situations and are separate emotional experiences. Both are related to the psychological state of *schadenfreude*, which is to rejoice at, or take joy in, or gain pleasure from the misfortunes of others. Can you see why this is an unhealthy emotion that must be stopped as soon as it is identified? Most times, wishing ill on others brings it on us, and this reason alone should encourage anyone to address any envious or jealous emotions.

People envy others for many reasons, and not all envy begins with malicious intentions; rather, it begins with a lack of self-esteem and poor self-image. As mentioned above, ultimately, an ungrateful attitude and lack of love for oneself can also produce envy. When one truly appreciates him or herself, his or her gifts and ambitions, that person begins to move toward setting goals using such gifts and ambitions. This action to make an ambition reality leaves no room or time for envy. Think about your goals and what you hope to accomplish in life and the gifts you have to make them happen. Most times, you will find that you need to only appreciate and apply these gifts or acquire skills to refine them. In short, focusing on yourself helps you to see what you have to achieve your goals, what you need to achieve them, and finally the course of action required to achieve them. Envy is an unhealthy and unnecessary response to feeling inadequate. Respond with a commitment to identify your skills, and your passions that can use those skills in a positive manner.

Sometimes, envy stems from ignorance or, more accurately, from an incomplete understanding of others' circumstances and feelings. Different lifestyles make certain things more accessible to some than it does to others. This is why talented musicians and artists must work harder when they don't have a family member in show business, while the daughter of music icons can put out bad music for years before she realizes it is not her gift. But working hard has never hurt anyone; in fact, it has built resilient and ambitious people that are difficult to beat because they never give up. When a person has made the decision to pursue his or her goals wholeheartedly, nothing will be able to stop that person—not even a person's envy or jealousy. Obstacles will become training tools, and opposition just builds the person's endurance. Money, status, or anything else that distinguishes people should never be a source of envy.

I believe that people can be socially sensitive and harbor bad feelings when they feel that they don't measure up to others. They may even feel embarrassed about it, resulting in jealousy. To be jealous actually says more about the jealous person than the object of his or her jealousy. The insecurity within that person is now put on display for all to see. The object of a person's jealousy simply exposes an insecurity he or she already had. Jealousy requires the person to actually admit that he or she feels inferior to someone else. Such jealous people almost "hate" the one their jealousy is directed toward for no legitimate reason. Again, it all stems from insecurity. Have you ever heard the saying, "My wife is jealous of my secretary?" This is a feeling of inferiority, either physically or intellectually. The wife feels threatened by the intelligence, relationship, or beauty of the secretary, and the secretary may not even be aware of it. Jealousy is never to be confused with admiration.

SELF-ESTEEM AND SELF-IMAGE

Poor self-image and lack of self-esteem make a person a prime candidate for envious and jealous emotions and actions. Parents and loved ones may not have built up a person's image of him- or herself as the person had hoped, and the result leaves the person feeling inadequate. Add to this feeling, so-called friends' statements like, "That will never happen. Dream on. What makes you think you can do that?" All of these statements can begin to further weaken a person's self image and soon he or she begins to question his or her ability and worth. Regardless of what you have been told or how you may feel, the facts are clear. You are unique, and there is no one else on the planet like you. Whether your mother has told you this, or your father wants you to believe it, is irrelevant. It is a fact even proven by science through DNA. No two people share identical genes; even identical twins have their own genetic code, unique to them. Think about this for a moment. This is why you can't be like so-and-so and why you should never desire to walk in someone else's footsteps. Your unique qualities give you exactly what you need to accomplish *your purpose*, and walk *your own* path. Once you grasp of this truth, you will never again allow envy or jealousy to take root in you.

Envy is also known as one of the "seven deadly sins" of the Bible. Everyone may be confronted by these sins at some point in his or her life, but it is our responsibility to overcome those emotions, recognize their cause, and push forward to live a good life.

People envy others for many reasons, but it is mostly because they feel other people are much more fortunate, smarter, more attractive, or generally better than them. They have falsely convinced themselves that they lack while others have. If you were to compare two friends where one is wealthy, well traveled, and well educated, while the other grew up in poverty, worked his or her way through college, and eventually landed a good job after hard work, which would you suppose is jealous of the other?

These two may be the best of friends and leave no place for jealousy, but one would assume that the poor friend automatically envied the richer friend. All of the main reasons envy surfaces are involved, but what if you were wrong? What if you found out that the rich friend always fought against envious feelings toward the poor friend because of the connection they had with her family? Or that the poor friend's ability to achieve success regardless of economic status was an object of the rich friend's envy? One might find this example silly, but it highlights an important fact that envious people fail to realize: What is valuable to one may have little value to others. While the rich friend can (seemingly) easily attain her goals, and the poor friend works hard, which do you think would place the most value on his or her achievements? This example should remind you that any time envy or jealousy attempts to spring up inside of you, it is your choice to embrace it or not. It also reveals the fact that close friends can envy one another for different reasons, while ignoring the blessings they themselves have.

How to Deal with Envy and Jealousy

Many people want to be approved of, based on their appearance, fame, or wealth. In an attempt to gain popularity, they expose themselves to the envy and jealousy of others. Some people envy what others have because they believe there should be a limit to what everyone should have, but that is not true. Referencing the example above, it is easy to see why the poor friend would envy the rich friend, but it is harder to understand why the opposite might be true. The root of envy comes from a belief that one lacks what someone else has. The poor friend may lack financial resources, while the rich friend lacks genuine love and affection from family and friends. Always wondering what people want from her, the rich friend finds it difficult to form lasting relationships and may even feel her own parents' substituted money for love. So you can see that there is no logical reason behind envy; rather, it comes from feeling lack and ingratitude.

Both friends can have a stronger relationship if they focus on the gifts they have and count themselves blessed for having them *and* one another. Instead of placing a magnifying glass on the other person's seemingly plentiful gifts, the friend should examine his or her own gifts, and how these can be used to bring forth the desired result (better relationships, more money, genuine friendships, etc). Envy reveals what a person finds to be important. But it can be a blinding revelation as it keeps the person from seeing what he or she *does* have and what he or she *can* contribute. No one has everything but everyone has something.

One type of jealousy refers to feeling threatened by a supposed rival regarding someone we love. People with low self-esteem are always comparing themselves with others. Never compare yourself with other people. Like *Desiderata's* Max Ehrmann once said, "If you compare yourself with other people, you may become vain or bitter; for always, there will be greater and lesser persons than yourself." What a true statement. We will always find people who have more or less and cannot gauge our successes or abilities by this. It is not what a person has that determines his or her greatness, rather what the person does with it. Intelligent people can waste their brains on drugs and alcohol, while less intelligent people burn the midnight oil studying for college. Do you think ability will overcome ambition in this case? Absolutely not. Use people for relationships. Relating to people and getting to know them will help you be grateful for what you have and, in the long run, maximize every gift you possess.

Remember, self-esteem has to do with liking who you are and making peace with yourself. It is about having a good body image and believing in yourself and your own abilities and capabilities. It is about knowing and acknowledging that the only person you can ever be is yourself and then working on being the best you can be.

When you spot jealousy or envy in others, including friends, family members, or associates, it is best to minimize your time with them if at all possible. Identify if someone longs to be like you or better than you, because the outcome of your relationship is unlikely to be positive. It is impossible to avoid all envious or jealous people in your life, but correctly recognizing it in yourself, and others, will aid you in making better decisions and better friendships.

Do not subject yourself to someone's negative emotions or constant complaining and whining. This is another sign of envy and jealousy. They may not have those feelings towards you, but they have them towards someone! Learn to recognize the "red flags" of envious and jealous people.

As mentioned above, envy also represents an ungrateful attitude. Ungrateful people often complain and whine about others but never take action to fix anything themselves. You have your own life to live; don't allow them to poison your happiness with their envious mentality.

I've learned not to hate, blame, envy, or criticize; rather, I have learned to appreciate what God has in store for me. That's right. The gifts inside of you are to prepare you for something, a mission, and a work. They are not given to lay dormant inside of you while you focus on others. Haters usually despise the people they wish they could be and resent what they cannot have. What a waste of time. You should only aspire to be you—a growing and more mature you as time goes on. Just as the famous Rev. Run of Run DMC says, "When people aren't grateful they become hateful." Choose your friends wisely and don't share your business with everyone willing to listen. Not everyone has your best interest at heart.

DIG DEEPER

To be envious is to regret one's failure to achieve good fortune or to despise the successes of others. It is often accompanied by a false sense of entitlement. Instead of working for what they want, envious people may believe they deserve it merely because they want it. Also, in their twisted perspective, they may imagine that the gains of others have been taken from them, so they are filled with resentment. The envious suffer twice: when they don't succeed and again when others do. Their negative attitude makes them unpopular, which further escalates their envy. Envy manifests itself in three stages.

The first stage is regretting one's loss. For example, you may have been in a golf tournament, beauty pageant, speech contest, or a political campaign, but despite your best effort, you may have had to watch someone else win. To feel a bit envious at that time is hardly surprising. As long as you lose gracefully, congratulate the winner, and wish them well, you should not feel ashamed. Occasional losses are helpful, since we can use them to develop our strength and character. This first stage of envy is harmless, but not so for the second stage. Failing to gain control and dispose of this emotion properly at this stage only escalates it to the next one.

The second stage is resenting the good fortune of others. This animosity may be expressed by ill will toward others. For instance, to increase our chances of winning, we may wish our golf opponent lands his ball in the sand trap. A beauty contestant may hope her rival falls off the stage during her dance routine, or a speaker may pray that his challenger freezes in fear and forgets his speech. A politician may hope the opposition drops out of the race because of a blunder or scandal he or she hopes to find. What's so bad about wishing our rival a streak of bad luck? After all, thoughts can't harm anyone, can they? Wrong! First, they can harm us by festering in our soul, for as the Greek Dramatist, Antisthenes, wrote 2,400 years ago, "As iron is eaten away by rust, so the envious are consumed by their own passion." Second, where do malicious acts originate? Don't they all begin as thoughts? That's what makes the second stage of envy dangerous. It has the potential of developing into the third stage.

The third stage is taking action to hurt others. So you see, if we're not careful, a little "innocent" envy can develop into hateful actions. This is why envy is treated seriously in the Bible: "Thou shall not covet thy neighbor's house; thou shall not covet thy neighbor's wife, or his manservant, or his maidservant, or his ox, or his ass, or anything that is thy neighbor's." (Exodus 20:17) Again, "A sound heart is the life of the flesh: but envy the rottenness of the bones." (Proverbs 14:30)

Those who act maliciously because of envy usually begin by criticizing and maligning others, and then by lying and spreading rumors. Although the envious are troublesome to others, they are also a torment to themselves. As they sink further into despair, they may begin to engage in violent behavior. Thus, envy can lead to hate crimes and more. Envy and its harmful results cause one to feel ashamed and may lead to self-loathing. Envy springs from a sense of emptiness or unworthiness, and the resultant thoughts and malicious acts are done to dull, soften, or conceal the pain.

How to Deal and Heal

Have you ever felt envy? I have certainly felt that way many times. I think that when we feel envy, we have the opportunity to become aware of our lack of self-esteem as well as work on areas that leave us vulnerable to this emotion. We only feel envy when we do not fully accept, love, or appreciate ourselves. Both envy and jealousy are toxic emotions, but they can be used to bring about healthy change.

To transform envy into a healthy emotion, we need to love and accept ourselves as we are and be grateful for who we are. We must also remember that envy is a symptom of ingratitude of our own uniqueness and self-worth. Always use this feeling to examine and improve yourself. Each of us has something to give that no one else can.

The cure for envy is goodwill, benevolence, and generosity. The secret is to focus on others instead of us. It is only by helping others that we will be helped. Is there someone you envy? The best thing you can do is to befriend them. When you express your admiration for their accomplishments, they will be happy to pass on tips on how you, too, can be successful. Instead of nurturing resentment, inspire yourself by their example and emulate their success. Focus on "How can I achieve that?" instead of "I wish I had that."

Use your negative emotions to help you grow. Life is like photography; we need negatives to develop.

If someone is envious of you and treats you coldly, try to be compassionate. The envious person may act cruelly, but it's not because he or she dislikes you but because the person is unlike you. Such people lack your strength. If they belittle you, they're just trying to cut you down to their size. Yet, if you extend your hand in friendship, you may have the power to change their life. By your own example, you will be able to teach them that blowing out another person's candle will not make their own shine brighter.

"I love the skin I'm in."

Have you heard the phrase "you must love yourself first?" I've heard it a million times before but never understood what it was really supposed to mean, until loving God and myself was all that I had left.

When you start loving yourself, you will begin to understand that whatever you want to experience in life—love, joy, peace, abundance, or health—you must first embody it yourself. When you love yourself, you want to share your love with others. Love becomes an extension of who you are. You do not have conditions in a relationship because you know you are prepared to offer unconditional love. I am only sharing with you what I have come to understand from God helping me through my own experiences. It is associated with our emotions and manifests itself in the chest area. *You might say that it is truly at the heart of the matter!* Loving yourself can be of great importance to your health. In fact, it should be the priority in your life. There is great joy to be found, and it resides inside of you. When you are enjoying yourself, you have joy within yourself. When there is joy in your heart, you are full of joy; you joyfully create your experiences, and you are a joy to be around. There are many great masters who walk the Earth and you are one of them. You are a master and you are a master creator. We are all master creators, but we have forgotten how much power is within us. Our core nature is love. "With great power comes great responsibility," was a line in the movie *Spiderman*.

I interpret this to mean that when you become aware of yourself as a spiritual being, there is great love for yourself and honesty in your character, which gives you power. With this power comes a responsibility to share it with others, so that they can mirror you and begin to love themselves as well. Envy is an opposite of love. Instead of using your power and becoming arrogant, as some do, you can influence others positively and be an example of what loving oneself look like. It does not mean you are responsible for anyone else or should attempt to carry another person's burdens. You are in control of yourself and no one else.

> *Influence others positively and be an example of what loving oneself look like.*

Count your blessings. Think of what you have, rather than focusing on what you don't. Live in each moment and treasure each one you can. Remember, it is true that some people are out to show off what they have, but envy is the improper response and only causes you inward turmoil. These people often have a great need to feel important and suffer from low self-esteem. Boasting and arrogance hides their insecurity. Have compassion for them; don't envy them. If you have ever dealt with envy or jealousy, I hope that this chapter has helped and encouraged you. Use it as a guide to map the root of these feelings and work on addressing them. When you can come to understand what you have to offer the world and understand that no one else can offer what you can, envy is an easy emotion to conquer. Work on you; focus on you.

If you have been the object of envy, do not allow this to make you arrogant or haughty, since pride is not the proper response, either. Arrogance is really insecurity in disguise and, just like jealousy and envy; it only hurts the carrier of the emotion, not the target. God made you for a purpose that no one else can fulfill, and He gave you every gift to fulfill that purpose. Meditate on this and leave the past behind.

I LOVE YOU.